KAREKIN I
In His Own Words

Iris Papazian

KAREKIN I
In His Own Words

Karekin I Theological and Armenological Studies Series

© Copyright 2002 by
Karekin I Theological and Armenological Studies Series

All rights reserved. Written permission must be secured from the publisher to use or reproduce any part of this book.

Manufactured in Canada

Digital photo restoration, design & layout by Khajag Zeitlian

We gratefully acknowledge the use of photographs from:
J. K. Hovhaness (New York), Harry Koundakjian (New York), Associated Press (Wirephotos), L'osservatore Romano (Vatican), Berge Ara Zobian (Boston), Eddy Masraff, Gillman & Soame (Oxford), John Taylor (Geneva), Keystone Press Agency (London), Dean Liambas, Cavouk (Canada), Varoujan (Beirut), Neshan Naltchayan (Washington, DC), White House (Washington, DC), Marc Van Appelghem (Geneva), Rouben Mangasarian.

To Hagop Didizian
1901-1978

Karekin I Theological and Armenological Studies Series
was established in memory of
His Holiness Karekin I
Supreme Patriarch and Catholicos of All Armenians
by the Haig and Elza Didizian Fund

Contents

Preface 13

Messages 17

Introduction 23

In His Own Words 41

Think and Enter 43

Karekin I 49
Supreme Patriarch and Catholicos of All Armenians

Karekin II 105
Catholicos of the Great House of Cilicia

The Journey Begins 157

Ecumenical Journey 181

1700th Anniversary 213

The Final Journey 223

Preface

*I*f I had to choose one word that personified His Holiness Karekin I, the word would be Hope. He was so full of hope, so optimistic. More importantly he was able to transmit hope to others. "Hope is a living power in us in so far as it reflects God's grace and mercy," he would say.

This volume, *In His Own Words*, is an introduction to an overall project which when completed, by the grace of God, will publish in a series the complete works of His Holiness, from the earliest days of his service to his last. *In His Own Words* is not meant to be a biography but rather a photo/narrative of his service and a celebration of his life. You will note that the volume does not progress in chronological order, but rather begins with his final and highest position as Catholicos of All Armenians, after the two introductory essays.

The project was born through a series of consultations amongst his closest friends initiated by Mr. Haig Didizian who knew that His Holiness wanted to be remembered through his works. The Catholicos was an avid reader and writer. The body of work he has left in three languages—Armenian, English, and French—is substantial. Thus far we have managed to bring together most of Vehapar's works, published and unpublished, including thousands of sermons, encyclicals, scholarly articles, speeches, lectures, forewords, and personal diaries from his early years. There remains one important work to be secured—his final work. In January 1999, six months before his death, Vehapar began a journal of daily meditations, which he had tentatively titled, "Life in Communion with God." The journal was always with him, even when he went to the hospital. I hope and pray that it will be found so that it can rightfully become a part of his legacy.

In selecting his words for this volume I have kept faithful to his style of writing, with minimum editing. I have kept his complex sentence structure because that is the way he wrote; when reading his words one can almost hear his voice. In segments that I translated from Armenian I have tried to keep his style and choice of words. As an example, although I prefer the English word, Catholicate, Vehapar never used that form. We often debated the Catholicate vs. Catholicosate question, but he never wavered.

At various times during his years of service Vehapar left hundreds of photographs with me, primarily for a number of books and publications I produced for him. The majority of the photographs used in this volume are from that collection as well as some obtained from the Holy See of Etchmiadzin, the Great House of Cilicia, the Eastern Diocese, the Eastern Prelacy, and family and friends. The task of reviewing, identifying and selecting from thousands of photographs was difficult and time-consuming. I made the final choice and take full responsibility for inclusions and omissions.

All of us associated with this project express thanks to His Holiness Karekin II, Supreme Patriarch and Catholicos of All Armenians, for the support he brought to this volume and his fatherly blessings for the overall project.

We are grateful to His Holiness John Paul II whose genuine love for Catholicos Karekin I can be perceived in the message he sent for this volume. They had immense mutual respect for each other that grew into a true friendship.

We also thank the Bishop of London, the Rt. Reverend Richard Chartres, for sharing his memories of the Catholicos with us.

We express our thanks and appreciation to His Holiness Aram I, Catholicos of the Great House of Cilicia, for his support by making the archives of the Catholicate in Antelias, Lebanon, available to us for research for the duration of this project.

His Eminence Archbishop Khajag Barsamian, Primate of the Eastern Diocese of the Armenian Church of America, gave his wholehearted encouragement to this project and provided his active assistance in various ways. We are also indebted to His Eminence Archbishop Oshagan Choloyan, Prelate of the Eastern Prelacy of the Armenian Apostolic Church of America, and His Eminence Archbishop Mesrob Ashjian, for their valuable support.

Thanks also to His Excellency Armen Sarkissian and Dr. and Mrs. Raffy Hovanessian; to Vehapar's brother Zohrab and sister Yester for providing photographs from the family's collection; to Diramayr Sirvart Sarkissian for providing us with Vehapar's personal archives from his early years; Arpi Tchebookjian, Haikanoush Mesrobian, Christopher Zakian and to Khajag Zeitlian who spent the better part of his weekends and evenings preparing the final design.

I am personally indebted to Dr. Vazken Ghougassian, my colleague on this project, whose judgment I value highly. Vazken knows Vehapar's life and work better than anyone. He worked with Vehapar for eighteen years in various capacities. A graduate of the Cilician Seminary, he was Vehapar's assistant in Iran and in New York, and Chancellor of the Holy See of Cilicia under Karekin II.

I don't know how to express my gratitude to Haig and Elza Didizian. There are no words. They are two of Vehapar's dearest friends. Their dedication to this project goes far beyond their financial commitment—it is a mission of love for them to which they bring their active participation. My words of thanks are not enough. They deserve the gratitude of all.

We were fortunate to be part of that generation to benefit from the life and service of Karekin Vehapar. We will never forget him. He brought us closer to God and made us proud sons and daughters of the Armenian Church. For the generations that follow, who will never see his sparkling eyes nor hear his impassioned speech, I hope the publication of his complete works will in small measure provide a picture of an extraordinary churchman who served his Lord and people with faith, hope, and love.

Iris Papazian
April 2002

ԾԱՅՐԱԳՈՅՆ ՊԱՏՐԻԱՐՔ
ԿԱԹՈՂԻԿՈՍ
ԱՄԵՆԱՅՆ ՀԱՅՈՑ
ՄԱՅՐ ԱԹՈՌ Ս. ԷՋՄԻԱԾԻՆ

SUPREME PATRIARCH
CATHOLICOS
OF ALL ARMENIANS
MOTHER SEE OF HOLY ETCMIADZIN

Untiringly with His People Worldwide

From the Mother See of Holy Etchmiadzin, we greet with heartfelt joy and warmth the publication of the anthology of Karekin I, Catholicos of All Armenians of blessed memory, dedicated to the 70th anniversary of his birth.

On this noteworthy jubilee, once again there emerges before our eyes the devoted and courageous shepherd, the enthusiastic instructor and the learned preacher, who spoke tirelessly to his people worldwide, led them paternally toward God, kept alive the love of Holy Etchmiadzin and the motherland in the soul of every Armenian and forged their hearts into a treasury of the ancient and rich Armenian culture.

Our people will always cherish the inspiring example of Catholicos Karekin's life, which was filled with faith and work, his priestly spirit of loyalty and strength and the heritage he left behind. His legacy consists of a generation of clergymen called to the task of educating the subsequent generations, newly constructed or renovated churches, delivered lectures and published books which testify to the time and the life of a unique personality whose vocation was service.

We firmly believe that the present published anthology of the late Catholicos Karekin in English is a condensation of his conviction and it will generate and renew faith and strengthen love toward God not only in the hearts of the children of our people, but also in the English speaking readers. It will also be informative and a source of wisdom.

With pontifical love, we convey our appreciation and blessing to Mr. and Mrs. Haig and Elza Didizian, the kind patrons of the publication of this anthology, as well as to all those who contributed towards this publication.

This book is a most fitting expression of paying tribute to the loving memory of Catholicos Karekin I. Let the word of the blessed Catholicos continue to guide and strengthen his beloved flock and may his righteous soul find its eternal rest with the heavenly Father.

"The eyes of God are directed at the righteous and his ears upon their prayers." (Psalm 34:15).

With blessings,

Karekin II
Catholicos of All Armenians

April 10, 2002
No. 359

ՍԱՅՐԱԳՈՅՆ ՊԱՏՐԻԱՐՔ
ԿԱԹՈՂԻԿՈՍ
ԱՄԵՆԱՅՆ ՀԱՅՈՑ
ՄԱՅՐ ԱԹՈՌ Ս. ԷՋՄԻԱԾԻՆ

SUPREME PATRIARCH
CATHOLICOS
OF ALL ARMENIANS
MOTHER SEE OF HOLY ETCMIADZIN

Թիւ 359 10 Ապրիլի, 2002 Թ.

ԱՌԱՆՑ ՀՈԳՆԵԼՈՒ՝ ԱՇԽԱՐՀԱՄԲՅՈՒՐ ԻՐ ԺՈՂՈՎՐԴԻ ՀԵՏ

Մայր Աթոռ Սուրբ Էջմիածնից հոգու բերկրանքով և ջերմօրէն ողջունում ենք հոգելույս Գարեգին Ա Ամենայն Հայոց Կաթողիկոսի ասույթների ժողովածուի հրապարակությունը՝ ծնված երանաշնորհ Հայրապետի ծննդեան 70 ~ամյակին:

Հիշարժան այս հորելյանին վերսին մեր հայացքն առջև հառնում է անձնդիր և բազ հովիվը, խանդավառ ուսուցիչը, հմուտ քարոզիչը, ով գիտեր առանց հոգնելու գրոցել աշխարհասփյուռ իր ժողովրդի հետ, հայրաբար առաջնորդել դեպի Աստված և ամեն հայի հոգում վառ պահել Սուրբ Էջմիածնի ու Հայրենիքի սերը, նրանց սրբերը զանգառան դարձնել հնագույն ու հարուստ հայ մշակույթի: Ընդմիշտ մեր ժողովրդի հետ են նրա՝ հավատով ու գործով լեցուն կյանքի ոգեշնչող օրինակը, հոգևորականի ուխտապահ ու արի հոգին և թողած ժառանգությունը: Նրա ավանդը հոգևորականների սերունդ է՝ կոչված նորանոր սերունդներ կրթելու, կառուցված կամ նորոգված եկեղեցիներ են, կարդացված դասախոսություններ, տպագրված գրքեր, որոնք բոլորը պատմուն են երախտարժան Հայրապետի ժամանակի, կյանքի մասին մարդու, ում կոչումը ծառայությունն էր:

Մենք հավատում ենք, որ Գարեգին Ա լուսահոգի Հայրապետի ասույթների անգլերենով հրապարակվող այս ժողովածուն՝ իբրև նրա հավատավոր խոսքի խրախում, ինչպես մեր ժողովրդի զավակների, այնպես և անգլիախոս շատ ընթերցողների հոգիներում նախ և առաջ հաստատելու և նորոգելու է հավատը, գործածնելու սերը առ Աստված, բերելով նաև ճանաչողություն և իմաստություն:

Հայրապետական սիրով Մեր գնահատանքն ու օրհնությունն ենք բերում ժողովածուի հրապարակության ազնիվ հովանավորներ Տեր և Տիկին Հայկ և Էլզա Տիփիզյաններին և բոլոր նրանց, ովքեր մասնակցություն են բերել հրապարակության իրականացմանը:

Գիրքը Գարեգին Ա Հայրապետի սիրելի հիշատակին մատուցվող խոնին հարգանքի ամենաարժանի իրագործումն է: Թող Երանյալ Հայրապետի խոսքը շարունակի առաջնորդել ու զորացնել իր սիրեցյալ հոգին, և թող նրա արդար ու աղոթախոս հոգին հավերժական հանգիստ գտնի մեր երկնային Հոր մոտ:

«Աչք Տեառն ի վերայ արդարոց, և ականջք Նորա ի վերայ աղօթից նոցա» (Սաղմ. ԼԳ, 16):

Օրհնությամբ՝

ԳԱՐԵԳԻՆ Բ
ԿԱԹՈՂԻԿՈՍ ԱՄԵՆԱՅՆ ՀԱՅՈՑ

To His Holiness Karekin II
Supreme Patriarch and Catholicos of All Armenians

With great respect and gratitude, I remember my last meeting with Catholicos Karekin I, which took place in Rome on 25 March 1999. Before leaving for Etchmiadzin, he addressed to me these words: *"I thank the Lord for giving me the profound joy of meeting you personally for the third time in my life, and for reconfirming and advancing the fraternity which we have commonly felt from our first meeting. I thank you for having made this meeting possible despite the difficult conditions of health which are currently mine. Our fraternity and communion surpass all barriers."*

You will understand then my joy when I learned that a publication honoring His Holiness Karekin I Sarkissian is being prepared and that you would happily accept a brief reflection on my part.

Fraternity and *communion* were indeed sacred words for Catholicos Karekin I. Wherever he exercised his pastoral ministry, he wanted to be like the Good Shepherd, bringing peace and reconciliation to his people. With patient love, he was a fervent promoter of the search for unity among all Christian Churches and Ecclesial Communions. Since the time of his presence as an observer at the Second Vatican Council, he made a considerable contribution to strengthening the bonds of charity between the Catholic Church and the Armenian Apostolic Church. Both as Catholicos of Cilicia and as Catholicos of Etchmiadzin, he visited me here in Rome. Indeed, we were joined by a deep bond of affection.

A milestone in our fraternal relation was the *Common Declaration* we signed on 13 December 1996, in which we expressed *"a particular pastoral concern for the Armenian people, both those living in their historic motherland where freedom and independence were once more recovered and re-established recently through the creation of the new Independent State of Armenia, those living in Nagorno-Karabakh in need of permanent peace, and those who live in a state of world-wide diaspora. Amid upheavals and tragedies, especially during this century, these people have remained faithful to the apostolic faith, the faith of martyrs and confessors, the faith of millions of unnamed believers for whom Jesus Christ the Son of God incarnate and Saviour of the world, has been the foundation of their hope and whose Spirit has guided them across the centuries."*

The richness of the spiritual stature of Catholicos Karekin I was particularly evident in the meditations and prayers which he prepared for the *Way of the Cross of Good Friday, 1997*. For the twelfth station, Jesus dies on the Cross, he wrote this splendid prayer: *"O Lord departed, we humbly beseech You: Stay in us, be with us. Without you we are in darkness. Breathe in us Your 'last breath.' May it become the first breath of our new life in You. Instill in us the mind and heart of the centurion, who with Your 'last breath' felt the overflowing breath of Your Holy Spirit and courageously confessed by saying: 'Truly this man was the Son of God.' Kneeling before Your cross we repeat: 'Truly You are the Son of God.'"*

It is my fervent prayer that the late Catholicos Karekin I may fully breathe in God's eternal love, that his life and his work may remain an inspiring example on the path towards Christian unity and that his writings may remain a source of wisdom and inspiration for generations to come.

To Your Holiness and to the entire Armenian Apostolic Church I express my heartfelt sentiments of esteem and affection in the Lord Jesus Christ.

From the Vatican, 11 April 2002

Ioannes Paulus II

The Bishop of London

Memories of Catholicos Karekin I

I see the Catholicos in my mind's eye holding a huge audience spellbound as he addressed the Ecumenical Christian Assembly in Graz in 1998. His speech revealed both the magnanimity and the humour of a gifted servant of God. He was able to quote from ancient Christian writers but also from the graffiti on the walls of the Camden Town underground station in London. His theme was a humane survey of contemporary culture and its relationship with Christian faith. Here was a leader deeply rooted in the tradition of his own ancient church but also a citizen of the world. He did not merely handle spiritual themes but in his own person he exemplified the divine beauty which is ancient but always fresh.

We were privileged to know someone who was a bridge between the Eastern and Western Christian worlds. It was delightful to entertain him in my house with some of the scholars who had become friends during his time in Oxford. The Catholicos had a proper dignity but he was never pompous and he put everyone at their ease. Like all those who have served in his office, he carried huge responsibilities for the whole Armenian people but his presence was not in any way oppressive. He was the perfect ambassador for the Church and people he loved. Rest eternal grant unto him, O Lord and let light perpetual shine upon him.

Richard of London

The Rt Hon & Rt Revd Richard Chartres DD FSA
132nd Bishop of London

Introduction

*I*n his inaugural encyclical as Catholicos of All Armenians, His Holiness Karekin I wrote: "We do not know—and cannot know—where we are going. That is God's work. Ours is a duty of response. But we know very well that what God knows and does is only for our goodness: for the goodness of both our individual and collective existences, which is the kingdom of heaven in us, the original fountain of unsurpassable happiness."

His Holiness Catholicos Karekin I, lived his entire life with complete faith in the goodness of God and he served his Lord as a dutiful son. He faced life and death with faith, hope, and love. The example he left will remain a great legacy for all of humanity and especially for the Armenian Church and nation.

***

*H*is Holiness Catholicos Karekin I, baptismal name Nishan Sarkissian, was born in Kessab (northern Syria) on August 27, 1932. He was the first born child of Hagop and Ovsanna Sarkissian. A brother, Zohrab, and sister, Yester, completed the family. After attending the Armenian Elementary School in Kessab he was admitted to the Theological Seminary of the Armenian Catholicate of Cilicia in October 1946. In a poignant essay written years later, His Holiness recalled the circumstances of his entrance into the Seminary. At age 14 he had decided to leave school, although he was a good student, because he felt it was his obligation to learn a trade in order to help ease the financial circumstances of his family. His Holiness relates: "It was a Saturday. A hot August afternoon. The village was just awakening from its noontime rest. A cool, light breeze had begun to gently blow through the windows and was making its presence known to the trees and the leaves. Did my father perhaps think this to be the most appropriate time? I don't know. But clearly I was being sought. He wanted to speak with me, alone…. 'Come sit here,' he said, in a tone of voice which told me he had something of great importance to say to me. 'What is this I hear that you do not want to go to school next year. What is the matter?'"

His Holiness goes on to relate his encounter with his father which resulted in his agreement to enter the Seminary. He was accepted into the Seminary in October 1946. On May 29, 1949, he was ordained a deacon and he graduated with high honors in June 1952.

His Holiness always spoke fondly of his roots in Kessab and would often relate how Kessab was linked to the exodus of Armenians from the city of Ani, the capital of the Armenian kingdom under the Bagratids. "In the eleventh century, the Seljuk Turks invaded Ani. A large part of the Armenian population left the country and found refuge in western regions and Cilicia. The origins of Kessab and Musa Dagh go back to that time. Musa Dagh, of course, is well known because of Franz Werfel's book, The Forty Days of Musa Dagh." His Holiness would confess, "until age thirteen I did not know that electricity existed." The family's modest home was right next to the church. In later years he would reflect that it was his childhood in Kessab that gave him his connection to the earth, and his grandmother, who he described as "very pious," his connection to God and God's gifts. It was in Kessab also where his love of books began. There was no television and not even radio. But he discovered books in the library of the local club and found that he could learn everything and "go everywhere" just by reading books.

On September 28, 1952, he was ordained a celibate priest, renamed Karekin in honor of Catholicos Karekin Hovsepiantz, a renowned scholar and religious leader, and joined the Religious Order of the Armenian Catholicate of Cilicia. "I don't know if it was a rational act to enter monastic life at age twenty. However, I did not hesitate. The desire to serve my church was so strong that I could not envision other avenues for my life. I had the motivation, and I knew that in our tradition monastic life did not mean separation from my people. In my final year at the seminary, I was so engrossed with my studies and my teaching that forming a family did not enter my thoughts. The zeal of my youth for service in the church surprised me in my later life. It was the spiritual and intellectual that had captivated me completely. I had personal and psychological difficulties, but I never seriously thought of retracing my steps. My colleagues and my students became my family. I was alone, but I was not isolated."

Upon presentation and defense of his doctoral thesis, *The Theology of the Armenian Church According to Liturgical Hymns*, before an academic committee of the Brotherhood he was elevated to the rank of Vartabed on June 5, 1955. He then assumed the duties of supervisor and member of the faculty of the Cilician See's Theological Seminary in Antelias, Lebanon. He was appointed Dean of the Seminary in 1956.

From 1957 to 1959 he studied Theology at Oxford University in Great Britain. The World Council of Churches had awarded him a two-year scholarship. Oxford, he often said, was a life-changing experience for him. It was an experience he often talked about almost with reverence and longing. Years later, during his tenure as Prelate in New York, he liked to walk in light rain because he would say, "It reminds me of Oxford." His stories about Oxford are many. It was his first adventure into Western society—indeed it was the first time he was out of Lebanon and Syria, and in a non-Armenian environment. He relates how he felt alone and isolated at first but then became challenged by a fellow student's inquiry, "Where is Armenia?" It was the first time that he realized that Armenia and Armenians were not household words. "I became determined to make Christian Armenia known as authentically and to as many people as I could. I felt I was carrying this great burden on my shoulders to make my country, my people, and my church known to all." Oxford, His Holiness said, also made him understand the Armenian Church in a new light. "While studying Christian history and thought more clearly, I realized that it is by no means a vestige of the past; it never became stagnant as some people believe. I have discovered, for example, that the missionary vocation and our efforts to spread the Gospel have always been present in our tradition, although they had been emphasized less because of certain historical circumstances. But it is necessary to study our Fathers more closely, to rediscover our spiritual heritage. Oxford—which for me meant contact with the Anglican, Catholic, Protestant, and Orthodox traditions— truly taught me the significance of my studies: to rediscover and reevaluate the latent forces in the Christian Armenian tradition."

In his own words written many years ago, the young Karekin Vartabed recalls, "I arrived in Oxford in October 1957. The main purpose of my coming to England was to further my studies in Dogmatic Theology and Church History. As I was already teaching the same subjects in the Armenian Theological Seminary in Antelias, Lebanon, I thought my studies at Oxford would help me to acquire a wider knowledge of these subjects for my later work in the Seminary…. I think I was very fortunate to be placed in Wycliffe Hall. This is a Church of England Theological College for the training of the Anglican clergy. The students here have easy access to the University lectures, which later proved to be extremely helpful to me in connection with my lecturing work in the Seminary…. At the end of the second term I was accepted by the Board of the Theological Faculty as a post-graduate student, a candidate for the degree of B.Litt. The subject of the thesis for this degree had to have an ecumenical significance. So I chose the following theme: 'The Council of Chalcedon and the Armenian Church.' In fact, as it is well known, the Council of Chalcedon is the chief, if not the only, cause of the separation between the Greek Orthodox and Armenian churches. The latter rejects the Council of Chalcedon, which is accepted by the former as the 'fourth ecumenical council.' So I decided to study the historical and theological reasons for the rejection of the Council of Chalcedon by the Armenian Church and to try to see a possible way of reconciliation between these churches."

After successfully completing his course of study at Oxford he received his B.Litt. (OXON) upon presentation of his scholarly thesis, "The Council of Chalcedon and the Armenian Church," published in London by S.P.C.K. in 1965 and reprinted in New York in 1976 and in Beirut in 1982.

Without doubt the two years that he spent at Oxford had a profound influence on his thinking, approach and vision. As he wrote at the time, "…I would say that after my experience and studies [in Oxford], I have begun to understand my own church, but this time in a different setting from that in which I had seen and known it until now. That new setting is the vision of the Church Universal. If we begin to see the vision, then, I am sure, we are on the way to its actual realization. The unity of the church cannot come, humanly speaking, until and unless this vision is seen and felt by all Christians."

Upon his return to Lebanon in January 1960, Father Karekin resumed his responsibilities as Dean of the Seminary. Under his dynamic leadership and wise guidance the Seminary flourished and new generations of clergymen, inspired by his own example, joined the ranks of the Cilician Religious Order.

The unexpected and untimely death of Catholicos Zareh in 1963 became a time of personal turmoil for Father Karekin. "I could not understand how someone so pious, so devoted, so good could be taken from us so suddenly. It was a test of my faith."

With the election of Khoren I to lead the See of Cilicia, Father Karekin helped organize the official visits of the Catholicos to Greece, the Vatican, the Archbishop of Canterbury, and the international headquarters of the World Council of Churches.

As one of the principal promoters of the ecumenical movement within the Armenian Church, he regularly attended inter-church conferences, consultations and meetings. He took part in the General Assemblies of the WCC of 1961 (New Delhi), 1968 (Uppsala), 1975 (Nairobi), and 1983 (Vancouver). At Uppsala he was elected a member of the Central and Executive Committees of the WCC and during the Nairobi Assembly he was elected Vice-Moderator of the Council, a position he held until 1983.

As an observer he attended the three consecutive sessions of the Second Vatican Council (1963-1965) and the Lambeth Conference of the Anglican Church (1968). In 1965 he was one of the organizers of the Addis-Ababa conference of the leadership of the Oriental Orthodox (non-Chalcedonian) churches.

Following his attendance at the first session of the Second Vatican Council in 1963, Karekin Vartabed wrote, "…We could do greater service to Christian unity and to our own traditions if we, the Eastern observers, were more numerous, more representative and more competent. To my personal impression, we did not meet fully the opportunities offered to us. Again, it would have been an act of realistic attitude to be there, in the very heart of Roman Catholicism, and see directly what was happening there and where we had to stand and what we had to do in the future concerning our relationship with the Roman Catholic Church."

Upon the invitation of His Holiness Justinian, Patriarch of the Romanian Church, he delivered a series of lectures in Romania. Within the context of the Commission of Faith and Order of the World Council of Churches, he took part in conferences, namely in Zagorsk (Moscow), Bengalore and Kotayyam (India), lecturing on theological issues.

"I have been involved in the ecumenical movement since the first days of my diaconate, when I was still a student. I followed the nascent spirituality of ecumenism, which emanated, for example, from Abbot Couturier of Lyon. My first ecumenical gathering was a meeting with the directors of Christian university movements in the Near East in 1955. I remember the great figure of ecumenism Willem Visser't Hooft, one of the founders of the WCC, whom I consider a spiritual father. With a prophetic spirit he predicted a renaissance of the ancient Eastern churches, and with all his means encouraged the young priests and lay theologians of the Orthodox churches. Then I met Father Florovsky, Professor Alivisatos, Father Congar, Cardinals Bea and Willebrands—those eminent figures of true ecumenism strongly influenced my thought, my ministry and my life. For me, ecumenism is a profound spiritual reality. It is an essential dimension of our Christian faith. Unity is at the heart of the existence and the works of the church. On the path to ecumenism there have been failures and setbacks, but they do not take away from the essential process of ecumenism. We should never be discouraged. We should remain in dialogue, in communication, in spite of all obstacles. Unity is an obligation that we have received from our Lord, and in spite of our weaknesses and human fragility. We should never renounce it. Unity is love. I believe that, above all, dogmatic, intellectual, cultural considerations, it is the universal love, this attitude toward God, to others and to us, that makes dialogue possible. What is important in ecumenism is not the process of theological exchanges, but the manifestation of this love."

A strong believer in training the youth for leadership and involvement in the religious and cultural life of the nation, he founded in 1963 the Armenian Church University Student Association, grouping students from various universities in Lebanon. His concern about attracting and keeping the younger generations were very much a part of his mission. His charismatic personality and his exceptional speaking ability brought together legions of youth that remained a faithful part of the Armenian Church. His understanding of the problems of the youth was perceptive, even when he was in his middle years. "The younger generations born and brought up in areas such as the Middle East, Europe, the United States or South America, have to be cared for in different ways and by different methods from those to which their fathers and forefathers were accustomed. Attention should be given to the particular conditions in which they live today. But at the moment no diocese in such countries can, on its own initiative, engage in any serious activity with a view to changing certain things which have been integrated in or associated with the church during the past centuries…. In this respect, the church as a whole should adopt certain principles and indicate certain general lines concerning church reforms whereby the particular dioceses in different countries may be guided in their actions…. The guiding principle in such action should be to cause no harm to the unity of the church, on the one hand, and to enable the church to render a more effective witness in the twentieth century, on the other hand."

During the years from 1960 to 1967 he served as Dean of the Seminary and still managed to find the time to lecture on theology, literature, history and culture in a number of schools and universities in Beirut, namely the T. Hagopian College, Palandjian College, Beirut College for Women (now Beirut University College) and the American University of Beirut.

In recognition of his intense activities and contributions, he was elevated to the rank of Senior Archimandrite on June 16, 1963, and was consecrated Bishop on January 19, 1964, by Catholicos Khoren I. He was granted the rank of Archbishop on April 26, 1973.

From 1967 to 1970 he served as Provost of the Cilician Catholicate which put greater administrative duties on his shoulders as well as the important charge of looking after the well being of the Brotherhood. Always a teacher, he continued to teach and lecture at the Seminary and colleges.

The 1960s and early 1970s were to be the most productive periods of Karekin Sarkissian's output of theological and scholarly works. Perhaps not coincidentally, this period was also the most intense time of his involvement in the ecumenical movement.

In 1971, Bishop Karekin was elected Prelate of the Diocese of New Julfa, Isfahan (Iran) where he served until 1973. There he promoted religious and cultural activities, thus greatly contributing to the spiritual renewal of the Diocese, particularly among the youth. The Diocese's museum was rejuvenated under his direction and the collection was displayed in a professional manner. The library was re-opened after decades of being closed, and its rich collection was available for scholars and non-scholars alike. He also reorganized and renovated the printing press, which is the oldest printing press in the Middle East, having been established in 1636. He purchased new modern printing equipment and began to publish needed books. A monumental publishing achievement was the beautiful Miniatures of All Saviors Monastery of New Julfa. The archives of the monastery, which dates back to 1605, was organized, classified and preserved. The establishment of a youth center with cultural and athletic programs attracted the young people. In addition he organized teacher conferences, lectures, and religious education programs.

In 1973 he began his service to the Eastern Prelacy of the Armenian Apostolic Church of America whose headquarters are in New York City. His arrival was received by the community with unprecedented enthusiasm. The "young, dynamic, Oxford-educated" Karekin Sarkissian was welcomed warmly. He worked diligently in promoting various activities and services in the United States and Canada for the benefit of the people, especially the younger generations that he was able to reach and teach. Although his tenure in the United States was to last a short time—barely three and one-half years—the impact he left was far-reaching as the Prelacy community became vibrant and dynamic. He organized a community-wide commemoration on the occasion of the 60th anniversary of the Genocide in a grand but dignified event with deep ecumenical overtones, which set a model for future commemorations. Thousands and thousands of people filled Madison Square Garden to hear the likes of Dr. Jorge Lara-Braud, Dr. Willem A. Visser't Hooft, Dr. Elgin Groseclose, Barbara Tuchman as well as high-level representatives from every sister denomination, and national political leaders. Archbishop Karekin described the purpose of the event as two-fold: first to provide a greater degree of consciousness for our own people, particularly the younger generation and second to address ourselves to non-Armenian circles, namely to our fellow American people and the international community in the religious, political and academic worlds. He was later to write: "The 60th anniversary, in fact, proved to be a moment of intense self-examination, self-assessment and recovery of the latent forces in our community. It is time for all of these new stimuli to be channeled structurally into activities through which our Christian faith, national consciousness and fundamental human aspiration for justice may be enhanced and maintained. A nation needs this moral and spiritual rearmament in order to face the challenges of social and political evils that men and nations, for their own and often narrow and exclusive interests, impose on other men and nations. A nation that has lost that consciousness of dignity, the imperative to maintain and promote it, cannot live long. I hope our young people, being motivated by such healthy challenges as the nationwide observance of the 60th anniversary, will go on finding the proper ways to manifest their Christian faith and national dignity as their fathers did through their own blood and sacrificial ways of life. The forms, the methods of action, may change in this constantly changing world, but the spirit should remain the same and should prevail above everything else."

On May 22, 1977, Archbishop Karekin was elected Catholicos Coadjutor of the Holy See of Cilicia in Antelias, Lebanon, to serve alongside the ailing Catholicos Khoren I, who died six years later. During the eighteen years of his service as Catholicos Karekin II of the Great House of Cilicia, he gave new impetus to religious education by establishing a special Christian Education Department to promote Christian values through public activities and literary productions. His beloved Seminary was given his immediate attention. He revitalized the teaching staff and courses and transferred the Seminary from Antelias to Bikfaya, the summer home of the Catholicate in the mountains overlooking Beirut. Antelias, although once a quiet suburban town, was now a bustling metro area, and His Holiness felt that the seclusion of Bikfaya was more conducive to learning. A new modern complex for the Seminary was built in Bikfaya. Every Wednesday, throughout his pontificate, he would drive to Bikfaya and spend the entire day at the seminary teaching classes and spending time with the seminarians.

The on-going civil war in Lebanon continued during His Holiness's tenure and he and his faithful people were to witness some of the darkest days in the history of the Armenian community of Lebanon. During the years of unending war His Holiness rallied his community to maintain hope—Living Hope. "How desperately we are in need of this living and life-giving hope here in the Middle East, and today as we gradually approach the end of the second millennium of our Christian history! Yes. We need it. But can we have it? If we carefully listen to the message of our Lord's teaching as expressed in His Gospel…we can acquire it if we open ourselves to the mercy of God, if we succeed in emancipating ourselves from the dominion of so many humanly created gods of purely secular ideologies, values and ways of life…. Living Hope is not a static reality. It cannot leave us indifferent, in a state of mind of 'sit and wait' on our dreams. As I said, it is a quality of life in which God's presence is the source of life and service."

Always "full of hope"…but still the conditions in Lebanon would at times seem to go beyond hope, as he wrote in a letter: "As I write these lines in my headquarters in Antelias, Lebanon, it will not be natural, neither is it possible not to share with you in the spirit of fellowship the heavy state of mind and soul in which we are caught up together with all the people of this country. Here, particularly in the last year, and at the time when these words are being put on paper, the Christmas season is cloudy. We are still wandering in the wilderness. The anxiety in the hearts of the people has reached a state of traumatic experience. Schools are closed. Normal conditions of life are disrupted. We earnestly look forward—it seems without any tangible sign of hope in the horizon—to re-tasting the sweetness of peace. But the sour bitterness is all around us. Join us as we once more eagerly turn our eyes to the sky in expectation of peace and concord, stability and recovery. As you offer your prayers to the Lord Incarnate at this time of Christmas, please add one word to your supplication: pray that peace be granted to the people of a land which is so close to Bethlehem where peace was proclaimed two thousand years ago, but from where, alas, peace is departed at this present time of the close of the second millennium of Christian history."

Through his leadership, the cultural role and mission of the church was promoted with special emphasis on publishing. The Cilician Press was modernized and computerized. During his 18-year tenure the printing press kept running continuously even under difficult circumstances. Hundreds of volumes were published. He organized an annual book fair encouraging the faithful to buy and cherish books. The book fair continued throughout the war years and continues to this day. A new Museum/Library was constructed—"A new house of light," he said.

Always cognizant of the need to modernize—he sought the latest technology for the printing house—yet he had reservations about the advancement of technology and would often express caution: "Today we live in such times where the achievements of man's scientific creativity, technological skills and industrial ingenuity have acquired such a dominant place and influence in our society that they tend to immensely reduce, even eclipse, the sense and the idea of God in our actual texture of daily life. Today's ways and styles of human life have acquired a character and a pace of galloping change and tremendously overflowing intensity, and unprecedented crowded content.... My beloved people... take a prudent and scrutinizing stand in front of the innumerable temptations of the extreme secularism of today's world. Such influences are a real threat to the integrity of our humanness."

Programs for the youth and with the youth received his personal attention. The social services of the Catholicate were promoted through his own visits as well as the active participation by clergy and lay people, both men and women, in the various activities of the World Council of Churches and the Middle East Council of Churches, of which he was a founding member.

His dynamic oratory skills resulted in many invitations by universities and churches; he traveled extensively to lecture on a great variety of subjects. In the last few years of his service to the See of Cilicia he undertook extensive visits within Lebanon, Syria, Iran, Cyprus, the United States, Canada, Kuwait, and the Gulf states. Within the framework of his ecumenical activities and duties he visited His Holiness John Paul II, Dr. Robert Runcie, Archbishop of Canterbury; the Federation of Swiss Protestant Churches; the Lutheran Church of Denmark; the Lutheran Churches in Germany; the Australian Council of Churches, His Holiness Pope Shenouda III, Head of the Coptic Church.

In 1989, having completed his term of office as one of the three presidents of the Middle East Council of Churches, he was elected honorary president of that organization. His service to the WCC included membership in the Faith and Order Commission, serving as chairman of various committees, and attending four general assemblies. He served on the Central and Executive Committees for fourteen years, seven as vice-moderator.

Recalling his years of service to the ecumenical movement, he wrote: "I was a sixteen-year-old deacon when the ecumenical movement reached its decisive moment in 1948, with the creation of the World Council of Churches in Amsterdam.... My real baptism in the movement took place in Beirut in 1955. There at the Conference of Christian Youth Leaders in the Middle East, I was able to see for the first time such great figures as Dr. Willem Visser't Hooft, Dr. Phillip Potter and others.... It was my first experience sharing prayers, ideas, meals and simple conversation with people who neither spoke my language, nor were familiar with my own church's life and liturgical experience. Yet I felt at

31

home with them."

Even before he became Catholicos His Holiness made frequent visits to the Mother See of Holy Etchmiadzin in Armenia. As Catholicos of Cilicia he visited Armenia both during Soviet rule and after Armenia regained independence. He witnessed the efforts and accomplishments of the Mother Holy See and the Homeland, often under difficult circumstances. In the aftermath of the earthquake of December 7, 1988, he visited the stricken area and expressed solidarity with Catholicos Vazken I. Indeed, it was during this time that a deep and true brotherly love developed between the two. Weeks following the earthquake the two Catholicoi came to the United States to mobilize awareness and support for the great task of rebuilding. Catholicos Karekin was elected a member of the Central Board of Directors of the All Armenia Fund, established by the President of the Republic of Armenia.

"There are questions to which our human intelligence does not have adequate answers…I know well the extent to which that earthquake was a horrible calamity, an extremely difficult experience. I know how much suffering it caused, since I went to Leninakan, from Lebanon, ten days after the catastrophe. I saw with my own eyes the despair of the mothers looking for their children, the lines of coffins, the ruins, the piles of debris. At night, when I went back to Etchmiadzin, I was in a state of indescribable distress. But before that general destruction, I understood that we should not let ourselves be overcome with despair, that we had to react immediately to work on the reconstruction, which I said the next day in celebrating the Liturgy in the Cathedral of Holy Etchmiadzin. In this way, I found the strength to move on from that state of spiritual prostration… I understand very well when you lose a person, who was dear to you, when you learn that someone has a fatal disease, you wonder why? There are many aspects of our lives that cannot be explained. When the clouds hide the sun, you don't really wonder why God is making it so; it is something that is a part of nature, part of the rhythm of life. Faith reveals itself precisely when our logic does not understand. So the question of why the earthquake happened, or illness, remains without a logical response for us; here, it is a matter of believing that God is present even at the lowest point of the test."

In a personal show of support for the survivors of the earthquake Catholicos Karekin offered his gold pectoral twin eagles which he always wore. In a spontaneous and moving gesture, he removed the pendant from his neck and placed it on the altar of Etchmiadzin while celebrating the Divine Liturgy.

In April 1995, Karekin II, Catholicos of the Great House of Cilicia, was elected Catholicos of All Armenians by the National Ecclesiastical Assembly and became Catholicos Karekin I of the Holy Mother See of Etchmiadzin, becoming the 131st occupant of the throne of St. Gregory the Illuminator and the first Catholicos of All Armenians to be elected in the newly free and independent Republic of Armenia. It was the first time in the church's history that a Catholicos of Cilicia became Catholicos of Etchmiadzin.

In his enthronement sermon he addressed the people and said, "I am certain that you all realize the unique and exceptional significance of this patriarchal election. For the first time in the twentieth century, the election was carried out—as now this solemn ceremony of enthronement is taking place—during a period when our fatherland exists as an independent republic. Armenia has been liberated from seventy years of totalitarian rule, and today a benevolent, democratic regime prevails in our fatherland. The Armenian Apostolic Church, which has entrusted me with the office of its first servant, is summoned—at this decisive transition in our modern history—to an imperative mission of salvation. Led by the fundamental teachings of an historical legacy established by God and transmitted through Christ, it is called upon to pour into the life of our people new, clean and abundant water from the fountain of the Holy Gospels and the sacred tradition of our fathers—namely the eternal truths experienced through Christ and transmitted through the Gospels, the moral principles of human living, and spiritual values.... Without the Gospel, our nation would be weak. The identity and character of our people will whither, if we do not revitalize ourselves with the holy legacy of our fathers.... Our Church is also the cement of our national unity, the power that nourishes and fortifies our strength. If we are alert and perceptive, we cannot avoid noticing the 'signs of the time,' which place us all, without exception, under the command of unity, solidarity, brotherhood and harmonious cooperation.... The new state of the present world and Armenian life recommend to us nothing other than the strengthening of the unity of the Armenian Apostolic Church. A new chapter has been opened in human history. A new chapter has been opened in Armenian life. And a new chapter cannot fail to open in the life of the Armenian Church. The chapter of controversies and clashes must be considered closed. The chapter of unity has been opened, and it is our common duty to foster harmony, so that the unity of the Armenian Church may shine brightly like the light of the sun."

"I was not born in Armenia. But Armenia was born in me. It was born from that day when the Armenian language resounded in my ears through the cradle songs of my mother; and when the vision of the alphabet unfolded before my eyes—the lifeblood flowing from ancient tomes, which turned to ink on my fingers. Today I have come home to my ancestral hearth; it is as if I have never been away."

His election came amidst great jubilation with enormous hope and promise. Alas, His Holiness was not given the time to fulfill his full potential. Nevertheless he leaves a rich legacy of guiding the church at a crucial and difficult time. "Before my election," he often said, "through my frequent visits to Armenia, I had a certain idea about the task for which our Armenian Apostolic Church was called to, particularly after the radical changes in Armenia…. But now, having assumed this new highest and heaviest responsibility I see the situation in a much clearer way…. Let us be aware of the danger we face…the rapidly growing influence of extreme forms of secularist mentality and ways of life, which are superficial, superfluous and ephemeral. These new values, new life styles are attracting and influencing the younger generation and alienating them to their own Christian heritage. If the church does not take responsibility in this field of Christian education, the existing vacuum will easily be filled by various sects who will be creating what I call a spiritual confusion or a kind of religious anarchy in the life of our motherland of Armenia. We do not intend to express dissatisfaction or criticism of others. We are called to accomplish our mission as the Church of Armenia."

During the four years of his pontificate at the Mother See of Holy Etchmiadzin, he guided the Armenian Church with wisdom and unfaltering devotion and he dedicated all of his mental and physical abilities, in word and deed, to the sacred task of spiritually reviving, strengthening and unifying the people in the Motherland, in Artsakh, and in the Diaspora.

With a deep-rooted commitment to duty, His Holiness set his eyes on that milestone event, the 1700th anniversary when Armenia declared Christianity as its state religion in 301 A.D.

"We have before us as our immediate and sacred task the celebration of the 1700th anniversary of the proclamation of Christianity as the national religion of Armenia—in other words, the official establishment of our Church. During the reign of our beloved predecessor, Catholicos Vazken I of blessed memory, and by the united decision of the heads of the Hierarchical Sees of our Church, a special procedure has been set up to celebrate this great event as one Church, in a dignified manner, which ought to be implemented without delay. This is a golden opportunity to strengthen the inner unity of our Church, and to fully assess its mission, through which we may offer a new luster to our renewed people, and a new vision for the forward-moving growth of our newly-acquired State, in Mother Armenia and the Diaspora.

"The seventeen centuries of continuous, unbroken and creative witness of the Armenian Church is the integral part of Christendom and of human history. The 17th Centenary celebration is an excellent opportunity to bring that witness under both national and international, Armenian and ecumenical, pan-Christian focus. Particularly in this present age of world communication where the encounter of cultures has created a multi-cultural trend of dialogue and interchange, such a worldwide knowledge and recognition of Armenian Christian culture of spiritual, theological, liturgical, literary and artistic nature and content is not only possible but also important for an integral understanding of the relationship between Christian faith and human culture…

"In a sense the past may turn into a force that may lead the young generation to a new conscientization of their identity as the torchbearers of the living and life-giving flame of the Christian faith which has proven indomitable all along the past twenty centuries. The young are not only the inheritors, but, as I said, the torchbearers, a generation not to look backwards to the past for a sort of consolation or empty pride, but forward with new vigor and vision for ever greater achievements, to carry on forward the flame that gave life to their forefathers. Therefore, the 17th Centenary should be converted into a kind of Pentecost for the renewal of our Armenian Church."

He wanted the 17th Centenary commemorations to serve a two-fold purpose: first and foremost he wanted it to be a time of rejuvenation and renewal for the faithful of the Armenian Church, to learn the traditions of the past, but firmly rooted in the present and looking towards the future. "Everywhere and on every opportune occasion, we Armenians declare with pride to the whole world that we are the first Christian nation. In what way are we going to justify that primacy? Will it be through rhetorical words and self-praising ambition? By no means. The glorification of the past does not mean to turn the past into an idol and burn incense to it. If we continue the glorification of the past to the extent of being filled and glutted with it and try to wear peacock feathers, we would be betraying the past. Do not lose sight that the past has not passed. It makes an impact on us as a source of inspiration for new achievements and renewed creativity. Life goes on. At the end of the 20th century, we are the carriers of that life. We represent a link in that chain, which represents our life stretched over the centuries and tending towards an indefinable future."

Catholicos Karekin looked forward to "that great day in the year 2001 when all the celebrations will culminate and come to fruition…. We are going to consecrate a new cathedral in Yerevan, built with the drops of sweat of all Armenians and will be a symbol of our 1700th anniversary." Although he did not live to see the completion and consecration, he presided over the groundbreaking, and guided the construction of the Cathedral which would seat a symbolic 1,700 people. His predecessor, Vazken I, planted the seeds, Karekin I nourished its growth, and Karekin II guided its conclusion. In the final analysis the Cathedral in Yerevan may very well remain as the most tangible symbol of the 1700th Anniversary celebration. Centuries hence Armenians will point to the Cathedral of St. Gregory the Illuminator in the capital city of Yerevan and say, This is the work of our forefathers in honor of the 1700th anniversary of Christian Armenia.

Karekin I filled every hour and minute of his all too short pontificate to render them effective and fruitful. Due to his efforts, the dioceses of the Armenian Church in Armenia and CIS countries were reorganized and new dioceses were established. In an unprecedented flourish of construction activity, many churches and monasteries that were in serious decline were renovated and revived, and even new churches were built, especially in areas where there were no churches.

A new generation of spiritual servants was educated at the Kevorkian Seminary, which was thoroughly renovated, both its physical structures and its teaching staff. He took a personal interest in the seminarians and assumed some of the teaching duties. The activities of the Center of Christian Education and Preaching were invigorated and expanded. With the help of benefactors he established the St. Mesrob Center in Oshagan—"a hospitable place for scholars and theologians," he said. The press of the Mother See launched an ambitious program of publications and many works of theological, spiritual, and Armenological nature were published. A number of exhibitions were organized in commemoration of the 1700th anniversary including in Moscow, the Kremlin, Greece, and the Vatican. In many other sites, scholarly symposia were organized. Pilgrimages were planned to various venerated sites in Armenia and abroad. A number of social development projects were introduced to overcome the economic difficulties in Armenia and Artsakh.

"Although I had not lived in Armenia before my election, I always had my motherland in my heart. There are two major tasks for me: to repair what was destroyed for the past seventy years by an aggressively atheistic regime, and to build the new conscience of a Christian nation in a free and independent country. It is easier to begin to build when there is nothing there rather than to restore a heritage that is so profoundly wounded, as is the case in Armenia. This transfiguration of our nation requires a spiritual, moral, humane and cultural reformation. A nation cannot exist simply on the basis of economic and political stability. It needs moral perseverance, and the source for this is the church. Another of my tasks is to keep strong ties with the Diaspora. I try to identify with the people, speak their language and show interest in their problems. This is not a strategy. Saint Paul was Greek with the Greeks and Jew with the Jews. The idea of an aloof and reserved Catholicos belongs to the past. During Soviet domination, the Catholicos was forced not to be with his people. My predecessor had an easier time traveling in the countries of the Diaspora than in his native country. A pastor has to be with his people." He made every effort to be "with his people"—a gesture that was new to the people in Armenia. He addressed the people on television on a weekly basis. Whenever he visited various parts of Armenia he would stop and talk with the people in the streets.

Because of the prestige he commanded internationally, His Holiness was instrumental in strengthening the ecumenical ties between sister churches and by means of numerous pastoral-pontifical visits he established closer relations between the Motherland and the Diaspora. His Holiness was an honorary member of the National Academy of Sciences of the Republic of Armenia. A prominent scholar, he was the recipient of honorary doctorate degrees from a number of academies and universities around the world.

From the earliest days, books held a special place in his heart. He himself has written dozens of major scholarly and theological books, and thousands of articles, sermons, reviews, as well as in-depth prefaces and introductions. Through the years he was responsible for the publication of hundreds of books by other authors. He used every means within his ability to transmit his love of books to others.

"The man or the nation who is cut off from the world of books turns into a dry wilderness where only thorns and thistles grow and snakes and scorpions thrive. Men and nations who live in the world of books turn their lives into flower gardens or orchards where life flourishes into brilliant greenery, abundant fruitfulness and joyous beauty."

"What is a letter? A sign on a piece of paper. What is a book? A pile of papers. The letter becomes alive when it meets the eye. The book vitalizes when it penetrates the soul. Yes, the book itself is an inanimate, uncommunicative object, but reading it sets the soul, the heart and the mind in motion. It imparts life, communion and emotion. It arouses aspirations and joy, sometimes anxiety, protest or revolt, other times, quiet enjoyment, meditation and searching. It may even lead to discovery and happiness. In short, reading defeats desolation, lifelessness, apathy and self-negation, because man himself is life and motion."

* * *

There are certain characteristics that are unique to Karekin Sarkissian. Unique is a word that should not be used often, yet it is the only word that adequately describes Vehapar's special talents. First and foremost he had a dynamic charisma which drew people to him. He had a unique ability to communicate with people. He loved people. When he spoke to you his eyes twinkled with interest, and at that moment you felt he was only concerned about you and the conversation. Twenty or thirty years after meeting someone, often briefly, he remembered the person, his or her name, and the circumstances of their encounter. This ability extended to children as well. Children loved his humor, his down-to-earth approach and his genuine interest in their lives. Today many young adults speak of their great love and respect for Vehapar—love and respect which began when they first met Vehapar many years ago when they were young children.

His intellect was so keen that he was able to grasp complicated concepts quickly and then offer explanations that could be understood by the common person. He was at once an intellectual, a theologian, a scholar, a historian, a writer, a teacher, and a humanitarian.

It has been said that "All readers are not leaders, but all leaders are readers." His love of books is well known and has already been described above. Still, it needs to be stated again because since the earliest days of his life, when he discovered the small library in Kessab, he was a voracious reader. And while it is true that the only personal possessions he cared about were books, books for him were not mere possessions. They were his continuing education and he shared them with others. He would read new books, and re-read old favorites, and would gain enormous knowledge. Reading for him was not a passive activity. He became engaged with the words, taking notes, underlining passages, jotting comments on the margins. The uniqueness of his reading was his ability to retain what he read. His photographic memory could recall passages verbatim.

It is quite unusual for a person to be both a good speaker and a good writer. Vehapar was the exception to this rule. His oratory skills are legendary. He captivated audiences in an instant and kept their rapt attention. He could speak equally well in Armenian, English, or French and he had mastered the art of speaking in two languages in the same speech, back and forth, without confusing the message or the audience. And, most miraculous of all, he did not have a speechwriter. He always wrote his own speeches. Often he delivered multiple addresses in one day, always taking into consideration the audience and its special needs. Many of his speeches were extemporaneous—another great talent of his—and were later transcribed from tapes. His successful use of language, finding the right word at the right moment was another unique talent.

In modern terms he was a "workaholic." He would be up and at his desk before anyone else, sometimes at dawn, and he would work long into the evening hours. His writing ability was as great as his oratory skills. He wrote with pen and ink in beautiful, readable handwriting, crossing out, replacing words, sometimes creating words, and editing until it met his approval. He found time to correspond with friends; sometimes it would be a long thoughtful letter, sometimes a few lines of greetings in his own script, written on his latest message or sermon. Even under the most difficult circumstances, in Lebanon during the war, or in severe physical pain, his pen and notebook were with him recording his thoughts, his fears, his prayers, his hopes, and his dreams....

* * *

His Holiness died on June 29, 1999, in Etchmiadzin. With an outpouring of tributes, he was mourned not only by Armenians worldwide but all of Christendom. He was described as "An Ecumenical Giant." One prominent theologian said, "Catholicos Karekin was a great priest and distinguished leader of the Universal Church. He was in the forefront of the ecumenical movement and a loving pastor and father to his people. I feel privileged to have enjoyed his friendship. His loss is mourned not only by the Armenian Apostolic Church but by the Church Universal."

But it was the common men, women, and children who mourned the greatest. They lost their beloved leader—a leader who was also a friend, open and accessible to everyone.

In 1977, His Holiness wrote, "St. Augustine spoke of the City of God. Are we true citizens of that City? Let us be so that we may contribute towards turning God's creation, the world of today, into the City of God with godly people as its inhabitants.... Our credibility will be measured not by the eloquence of our words but by the quality and power of our life...."

The "quality and power" of the life of Karekin Sarkissian will surely live on, inspiring generations again and again to "carry on forward the same witness today and for ever."

Iris Papazian

IN HIS OWN WORDS

Think and Enter

It was a Saturday. A hot August afternoon. The village was just awakening from its noontime rest. A cool, light breeze that had begun to blow gently through the windows was making its presence known to the trees and the leaves.

Did my father perhaps think this to be the most appropriate time? I don't know. But clearly I was being sought. He wanted to speak with me, alone. His normal serious facial expression had taken on lines of worry and he was obviously distressed.

The minutes grew longer as he sat uncomfortably on the balcony of our house gazing at the school and church and toward the horizon to the gardens and vineyards visible through the small alleyway that separated the church and school from our house.

"Come sit here," he said, in a tone of voice that told me he had something of great importance to say to me. "What is this I hear that you do not want to go to school next year. What is the matter?"

I was a young boy of fourteen. I had completed my primary education in the village school. I excelled in school: successful in my studies and well liked by my teachers. But…I had decided to leave school and pursue a trade. I had already spent the three months of summer the last three years working with the village's best tailor—Serop Ayanian, nicknamed *Babayigid*. I was prepared to exchange my bright student days to be a student of a trade….

"Father, what can I do? When I graduate from school in two years what can I do with the education I have received? What good is that education here? The school has also begun to weaken. One by one the students of the

Nishan Sarkissian at six months of age, in Kessab.

43

school and village are going to Beirut. So, I decided that I would learn a trade. At least I will then have a job in the future."

A general view of the village of Kessab, His Holiness's birthplace.

I was not sincere. My father, an experienced man, immediately took note that there was something else hidden in my mind.

"First complete school, then we will see…," he said abruptly.

"Don't insist. It is impossible for me to continue school."

My father did not have a job. He had never farmed. He had served as a waiter in the village's club, but left that job. During the war years he had gone in the vicinity of Tripoli where he worked as a storehouse guard for the English regiment. That had also ended with the war and now he was unemployed and suffering. The financial state of our family was getting worse each day. He did not want this to be known, however with a sense of the dignity of a villager and the singular sense of a young man, I felt his torture. Coffee and cigarettes, so plentiful, made his inner turmoil so transparent…. In my short-sighted mind I thought that by learning a trade in the village and by earning one or two dollars a week I would succeed in helping my family and lessen my father's burden.

"Look, my son, I know why you don't want to go to school. It is true that our situation here during these days is not good. I sense that you realize this and you want to cut short your education in order to help me. For the love of God, don't add to my torment. Your education does not cost me one penny. You are first in your class and in the school. Recognizing your status as an excellent student, the school provides you with a full scholarship. The cost of your education is not a burden on me. You have earned it. For the love of God,

The site of His Holiness's home in Kessab. This photo was taken in 1991 during a visit to Kessab.

set aside your desire for a trade, continue your school and lift this heavy burden from my heart."

My mind was made up, my decision was sitting on my brain like lead. I could not see the wisdom of continuing my schooling. What good was my education in the village? It was a road which when completed would not open any horizons for the future. A type of blindness…a blind alley which when you reach the end, you wonder why you are there, and where you are going. The land. The farm. A trade. Is this worth eight years of education? A little farming work, a little tailoring…this is the sphere of my life, I thought. It was better to excel at these rather than find myself destitute and unable to find success in that environment.

During the summer many people came to the village for a change of climate, especially from Latakia, Aleppo, Egypt, and sometimes Beirut. Well-dressed, sophisticated people. But they came from the city. Here in our village what good was education? Could our villagers be like them? It was fate. With my natural inclination, without giving it thought, I had accepted my existence as a village boy. I loved books, but I could not make a living with books. Land and a vocation were going to be the center of my life. We did not have much land. A few small pieces here and there—vineyards and gardens, and one or two pieces of vegetable beds that suffered from lack of water. If I learned a trade along with the farming, I felt I had secured my future in the village.

But all of this, I realize now, more than being logical and thoughtful, was the impact of the times and environment on my young soul. My father had not erred.

In my juvenile zeal, my immediate goal was to earn money and help my family. I did not think that this type of reasoning could wound my father's self-esteem and cause additional heartbreak and anxiety to his growing inner turmoil. And, so, I relentlessly insisted on my decision.

Nishan Sarkissian in Kessab, looking very cautious and concerned.

Just as we—father and son—were engaged in a hot and bitter struggle, suddenly the village priest, Der Movses, went past our houses' balcony and toward the narrow street separating our house and the church. He was a beloved clergyman and very close to our family. My father did not attend church on a regular, or frequent, basis. But he was a friend of the priest. He liked to hear the church hymns at home, especially *Aravod Loysou*, and the hymns sung each morning and evening. The close proximity of our house to the church seemed to weaken the concept of attending church. But I, with the daily reminder by my mother, did my father's duty as well…by taking part in the rituals of the church. The readings, censing, singing hymns—all were very pleasurable for me. And because of this the priest showed special love and attention toward me. I helped to alleviate his loneliness in the church and also made his duties easier.

My father, apparently disillusioned in his attempt to convince me, made one final desperate attempt by calling out to the passing priest as though he, like swift Saint Sarkis, was heaven sent.

"Der Hayr, come here for a moment. Come have some coffee."

The Der Hayr came up to our balcony. He barely had sat down when he noticed the sadness in my face.

"What is it, Nishan? Are you upset, are you ill?"

I remained silent. What could I say to him? That my father and I were arguing? That would be shameful. It was better to remain silent, especially in the presence of my father. I also felt that if I revealed the subject of our conversation, Der Hayr would certainly agree with my father.

My father, convinced he had an ally, opened the conversation.

"Der Hayr, please make this boy understand. He has decided to leave school this coming year and become an apprentice to *Babayigid*, to learn tailoring. How can this be?"

"What is the problem, Nishan, are you not satisfied with school? Education does not speak to your heart? I, too, am amazed at this extraordinary decision of yours. Be assured that your teachers will also be very disappointed."

I collected all my thoughts and began speaking like an attorney. Well-organized and logical answers, at all cost, to support and justify my decision.

"For what sake," I said, "for what purpose should I continue my education? You know very well the situation of our village. Some of my friends leave and go all the

Nishan Sarkissian at age sixteen takes part in Parsegh Ganatchian's Choral Group. This photo was taken in Kessab in 1948. Vehapar is third from right on top row.

way to Beirut to learn a trade under better circumstances. I do not have the means to go. The village is my life, and it is not possible to earn a living here with education. You know very well the economic situation of my teachers. What am I to do with an education when I know it will be like a bird without wings? I beg you, Der Hayr, explain this to my father. Let him not be upset. Let him not be alarmed. His fervent disappointment tortures me also."

Der Hayr stroked his beard. His face took on a thoughtful expression. And then as though finding a solution, he said in a firm, convincing voice—

"Good. Since you do not want to continue this school, let us send you to another school."

"Where?" I said quickly.

"Antelias."

"Where is Antelias?"

"Near Beirut."

"What will I study?"

"You will receive a good education," he said. So as not to lose my interest he quickly added, "After you receive your education, if you wish you can become a clergyman. If you choose not to, you can become a teacher or an intellectual and eventually serve in schools of higher education."

"Fine. I'll go," I said and immediately looked at my father. The lines on his face suddenly receded and a smile—not seen very often—spread across his face with the look of satisfaction.

To this day, I do not know whether the words, "Fine. I'll go" were born in my mind or whether it came from the depths of my inner self, stronger than logic, which sometimes manifests itself like a calm and quiet flowing spring and then suddenly spurts forth like a torrent."

As a toddler in Kessab.

And so it was. Was it a chance occurrence or a pre-destined incident? I do not know. I left Kessab, the village of my birth, and went to Antelias....

Like so many before me, I read on the façade of the Seminary the words carved in marble, which glowed like gold, *Khoreh yev Medir*, "Think and Enter."

I entered.

But...I did not think.

***

Could I have possibly known what the Seminary was, and what was expected of me, or what I expected of the Seminary and myself?

But...I entered.

Years went by. From year to year I could clearly feel that the six years of my educational and student life became a rebirth for me. The Seminary had a special atmosphere. It was a way of life, a way of working, a process of communion. It was a lively means of inner fulfillment and maturity. It was God, Christ, the Bible, the Gospel, Hymns, Psalms, Classical Armenian, Modern Armenian, and other languages. Armenianism blossomed from the pages of literature and history and art and culture shone like the beacons of a lighthouse. It was enlightenment through theology and philosophy, with their various ramifications, prayer and study, exercise and work, experience and training — all connected to intellectual and spiritual work. Still other activities related to all these flowed into my being and captivated my entire life. And the village boy, although remaining as himself, added on new layers, and lived in a new arena—an arena which opened up new and wider horizons. And he wanted all of this to be channeled into the life of his people—including his fellow members of the Cilician Brotherhood, who had the same access as he, as well as for the enrichment of the people in general who had less.

The desire for a trade disappeared, transformed into a sweet memory...

The village's gardens and vineyards remained in me, but in a different form, in a different capacity and space. The gardens became the "small nation" and the vineyards became the vineyards planted by our Creator in which I served as a cultivator, beyond self and above narrow and personal circles.

The Seminary became, and remains in my life to this day, a "trade school of culture"... spiritual... national... educational...cultural, and social. Under the spiritual guidance of His Holiness Karekin I Hovsepiantz, the instruction of Archbishop Terenig, the erudite teaching of Puzant Yeghiayan, Shahan Berberian, Simon Simonian, and many other clergy and lay lecturers and mentors, I became captivated with the world of service, which became the reason for my existence. I knew that this would bring me happiness and meaning to my life.

And, finally, after six years of religious and intellectual training together with an Armenian "abode," I entered the field of religious service with new trimmings, and with a new name—a sacred name with a heroic posterity. This time I entered, *Thinking!*

Translated from the volume, *Khorhe Yev Medir*, published in 1984, Antelias, Lebanon.

KAREKIN I
Supreme Patriarch and Catholicos of All Armenians

I am certain that you all realize the unique and exceptional significance of this patriarchal election. For the first time in the twentieth century, the election was carried out—as now this solemn ceremony of enthronement is taking place—during a period when our fatherland exists as an independent republic. Armenia has been liberated from seventy years of totalitarian rule, and today a benevolent, democratic regime prevails in our fatherland.

The Armenian Apostolic Church, which has entrusted me with the office of its first servant, is summoned—at this decisive transition in our modern history—to an imperative mission of salvation. Led by the fundamental teachings of an historical legacy established by God and transmitted through Christ, it is called upon to pour into the life of our people new, clean and abundant water from the fountain of the Holy Gospels and the sacred tradition of our fathers—namely the eternal truths experienced through Christ and transmitted through the Gospels, the moral principles of human living, and spiritual values. It is imperative that these are poured to irrigate the orchard of Armenian life in the fatherland and abroad....

Without the Gospel, our nation would be weak. The identity and character of our people will whither, if we do not revitalize ourselves with the holy legacy of our fathers.... The Mother See of Holy Etchmiadzin—this holy sanctuary built by God and established by Christ—must, with God's help and through the dedication of us all, become a source of spiritual nourishment, which through generous irrigation will deliver the Gospel's "living waters" into the daily lives of our people....

The dream of previous generations has come to life. For the first time in this century, the president of an independent Armenian state is present with his state officials during the

Catholicos Karekin I under the Pontifical Canopy being escorted by the clergy and canopy bearers, 1995.

enthronement of a catholicos. I believe that our land, which is daily registering increasing stability and progress, will enter the third millennium with greater strength in order to continue its creative path towards the future....

We cannot be what we were. We are no longer a tributary people. We are on our own native soil. Once, we were mere communities scattered unto the Four Corners of the world, living under circumstances peculiar to a Diaspora. But the time has come for us to reform—to comprehend the value of a homeland and a national state. We are no longer just a Diaspora; now we are an independent state, a self-ruling and democratic people. Yes, we do have a Diaspora, and we will continue to have one. Millions of Armenians live outside their fatherland in a Diaspora state, and they have a great importance for all Armenians....

My brothers and sisters, it is necessary to build a golden bridge to span the distance between the fatherland and the Diaspora. We must remain connected in the geography of our spirit, kindling within our hearts the feeling that we are citizens of a single nation... With this same understanding, our Church must play its national role, since it is inextricably bound to the entire history and fate of the Armenian nation.

May the arm of Almighty God protect the entire Armenian people in the fatherland and abroad. Let us pray that God will tend to me as a shepherd, so that I may likewise tend as shepherd to you, His flock, in a place of green pastures, and beside the still waters, where He has made me to dwell, for the glory of God, for the tranquility and abundance of the land, and for the prosperity of the Holy Church and the Armenian nation.

Enthronement Sermon, 1995

The Enthronement Ceremony in Etchmiadzin, 1995. At left is H. E. Archbishop Karekin Nercessian (now Karekin II, Catholicos of All Armenians); at right is H.E. Archbishop Khajag Barsamian, Primate of the Eastern Diocese of the Armenian Church of America

The National Ecclesiastical Assembly which elected His Holiness Karekin I, the 131st occupant of the throne of St. Gregory the Illuminator, April 1995.

The Armenian Apostolic Church is here today with one heart, one soul, one will, and one vision. I speak for everyone when I say this is one of the most joyous days in our history.
Sermon at Consecration of His Holiness Aram I, 1995

During the last seventeen centuries, the voice of Holy Etchmiadzin has resonated through the prayers, words, letters, visits and leadership of 130 catholicoi. Today, that voice resonates through our humble person, as the 131st link in the chain of God-pleasing and nationally-elected catholicoi—who day and night turned their lives into lamp-oil made of tears, to keep the lamp of St. Gregory the Illuminator ever-shining as the guiding light of the life-journey of the Armenian people....

To the centuries-old Holy See of the Catholicosate of the Great House of Cilicia—which was the initial source of our own spiritual formation and nourishment; in whose religious order we spent forty-four years as a member and a servant; and where God granted us the privilege of being the Catholicos for the last eighteen years, we express the warmest feelings of spiritual attachment to it.
Inaugural Encyclical, 1995

As long as the Armenian wears the Holy Chrism on his brow, its glitter will be like a light to his path, and as he wanders in strange lands the dust of alienation will not soil his brow. His path will be straight, his steps firm and unyielding.
Etchmiadzin, 1995

Above: Catholicos Karekin I officiates at the consecration of His Holiness Aram I, Catholicos of the Great House of Cilicia, July 1995.

Right: Washing of the Feet ceremony in Holy Etchmiadzin, 1997.

Armenian Christian tradition as expressed through centuries of unbroken continuity is not a *tradition of isolation*, grown by itself and confined to the boundaries of its own national existence. It has emerged and developed in association and inter-relationship with and under the influences of other Christian traditions, such as Syriac, Greek, Georgian, Latin traditions, to mention the most important ones.... Armenia from the very beginning of the Christian era was part and parcel of the missionary, spiritual, theological, liturgical and cultural life and heritage of the early and medieval *oikumene*.... Armenian Christian tradition for me provides an existential illustration of the victory of faith and life over despair and death.

    The Armenian Christian tradition, although rich in history, is not reduced to history. You cannot study it only in historical archives and museum walls and shelves or in ruined remnants of cultural monuments or in the pale pages of ancient manuscripts. It is a living, on-going tradition that today inspires and nurtures about eight million Armenian Christians who live in their own motherland of Armenia, only one part of historical Armenia, and in the widespread world Diaspora....

    Today the Church in Armenia faces a new challenge of tremendously decisive and crucial significance. Towards the end of this 20th century, Armenia has reached its "finest hour" by having recovered its freedom and independence that were lost for so many centuries. We have just come out of a kind of 70 years of captivity under the Soviet oppressive and aggressively atheistic rule. No one can visualize and weigh fully the damage that has been inflicted upon the Christian churches under Soviet rule unless one lives there with some length of time and personally witnesses the consequences of a well devised policy aimed at

The golden arm of St. Gregory is taken by procession to be used in the blessing of the Holy Chrism (Muron), Etchmiadzin, September 1996.

The Holy Chrism is being blessed, with the participation of the church hierarchy, bishops, and clergy.

the eradication of the Christian faith from the country and elimination of the Christian prints, habits, customs, observances, from the public life of the people....

The church today is called to a new responsibility of bringing back to life what was tried to be enshrined as *historical monuments* of the past heritage....

When I see our liturgical traditions so often emptied of its life and reduced to sheer texts, the scholarly studies of their literary richness cannot give full satisfaction to my concern and desire of seeing it reacquiring its living and life-giving force within the life of the people for whom it was destined.

What I am trying to say can be summed up in one brief statement: Armenian Christian tradition has to come back to life if we want our country to be faithful to its past, to assure its continuity as a Christian nation and to buttress the new Republic with sound and solid moral principles of human life.
Lecture, 1996

*His Holiness blesses the chrism in the large cauldron.
The Catholicos is holding one of the relics of the church,
the Holy Lance with which Jesus Christ was speared on the cross. 1996.*

*...*Many sects have appeared during the course of our history, but all came like the wind and perished like the wind. Alien churches preached strange doctrines in a thousand and one manners, but they could not obstruct nor shake the pure and clear faith of the Armenian Church, the faith preached in Armenia by the Apostles, sealed by the Illuminator and flourished by the teachings of our Holy Fathers. The educational mission of the Armenian Church remained undefiled and irreplaceable.

Etchmiadzin, 1997

Yes, we must feel ourselves "a new nation," "a new people," not in the sense that we are just born. No! We are like an age-old oak tree. But we are new in the sense that now we have acquired and act with a wakeful awareness to be the masters of our identity and self-respect, and to ordain the course of our lives with our own minds and hands according to our faith, ideologies and our will.

Etchmiadzin, 1998

There will be thousands of people facing you and when you begin to sing the Lord's Prayer, only a few join in. They don't know the words, but you can see that they are with you. The majority of the people do not know how to cross themselves, but they try and they want to learn. We must begin by teaching them the very basic fundamentals, but we must also teach them the role of Christianity in their daily lives.

Taped conversation, 1999

His Holiness visits Khor Virab, the site of St. Gregory's imprisonment.

In the depths of Khor Virab (deep pit) with (from left to right) His Eminence Archbishop Karekin Nercessian, Very Rev. Father Krikor Chiftjian, His Beatitude Archbishop Torkom Manoogian, His Holiness Catholicos Aram I of the Holy See of Cilicia, His Eminence Archbishop Oshagan Choloyan and Very Rev. Father Vrouyr Demirjian

Related to this feature of the role of the Armenian Church in the development of national identity, is the character of what I would call tenacity that the Armenian Christian tradition displays so distinctly. The Christian faith, it seems to me, has played a very determining role in the preservation and unbroken continuity of the Christian witness in Armenia in the face of so many and so perilous threats by non-Christian forces, invasions and persecutions. From the time of the Arab Muslim conquest of Armenia to the times of the Seljuk, Tatar, Mameluke, and Turkish Ottoman dominations, Armenia passed through innumerable moments of *Gethsemane* and *Golgotha* experiences of temptation, trial and tribulation. And yet it did not succumb. The last and most deadly episode of such times of crucifixion was the genocide perpetrated against the Armenian people during the First World War.
Tradition: Living and Life Giving, 1996

To be living dead is more dreadful than real death. The martyrs of Der Zor are dead; nevertheless they are alive. We must not become living dead in our lives. Let us become conscious and renewed. Let us be strengthened in our faith and become like a sponge, so that when someone gets hold of us and squeezes us, only faith and love may come forth from our souls.
Etchmiadzin, 1995

Above: His Holiness with the people of Armenia.

Right: Walking to the Martyrs Monument, Dzizernagapert, with President Levon Der Bedrossian, and other leaders, April 24, 1995.

The days of a Catholicos being cloistered are over. We must go out to the people; we must be accessible to the people. In one year's time I visited our communities in Russia, Ukraine, Lebanon, France, Canada, the United States, Switzerland, and England. In May of 1996 I visited Turkey and I saw the intense spiritual commitment of our community in Istanbul. I was very pleased. While some of our very westernized communities—where there is much more freedom—have lost touch with a very old church, in Istanbul, the people are truly connected to the church and its teachings.
Taped conversation, 1999

His Holiness with the Ecumenical Patriarch, Bartholomew I, in Istanbul, May 1996.

I am very convinced that contact between nations and cultures is always positive. The greatest civilizations were born at cultural crossroads, and they are the result of the meeting of different cultures. The "dialogue between cultures" that people talk about so frequently today constitutes the path toward peace and the well being of humanity.

I think that if there is a difference between the beginning and end of our century, it's that today we must have a clear awareness of the fact that war and isolation lead nowhere, and that peace, understanding, and cooperation are the key to happiness. Human values are never contained within a single culture; such an absolutization would lead to catastrophe. I think that to truly feel one's affiliation to a country, and its uniqueness, requires an acceptance of others and their sense of affiliation to their own countries.

Between Heaven and Earth, 1999

*W*ith fatherly care and love, we greet all the civil servants of our state—from the nationally-elected and honorable President, to the members of the National Assembly, the government administration, the army and all government officials—by appreciating their dedication, during these most difficult and decisive conditions of our time. We hope and pray that awareness of vocation, patriotism and broadmindedness, honest and selfless attitudes toward building of the nation will lay further roots, will indestructibly strengthen the achieved independence, and will develop the life of the people, by the creation of normal conditions of life in the fatherland, with the full and generous participation of the entire Armenian nation.

Above: Visiting the President of Georgia, Edward Schervanzade.

Right: His Holiness congratulating and blessing Armen Sarkissian, shortly after he was appointed Prime Minister, October 1996.

Let us not forget that we have come out of the fire of death-spreading genocide, and for eighty years have been armed with a will to survive. Let us not forget that today the just struggle of the Armenians of Artskah is in need of all our prudent and vigilant attention and strength. Let us not forget that the just struggle for the rights of our people is the sacred legacy of our martyrs. For the sake of all these, the strengthening of the dignity of our national identity is our common and noble duty.
Inaugural Encyclical, 1995

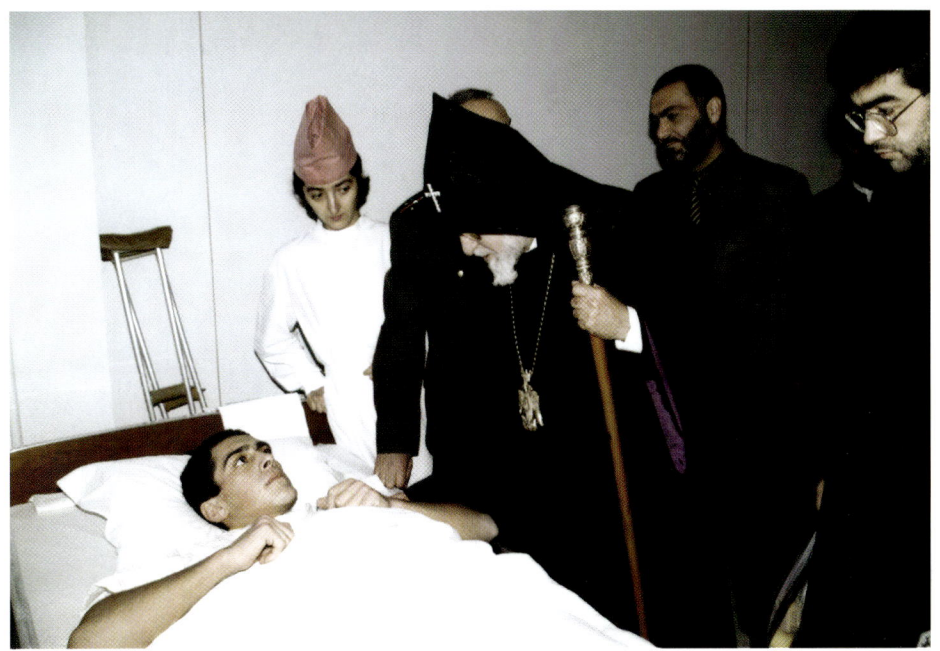

Visiting soldiers wounded in the defense of Karabagh.

His Holiness interacting with the young people of Karabagh.

*F*or the Diaspora, the Church remains a source of spiritual nourishment. However, at the present, secularism has become the dominant way of life. Fortunately and thanks to the honorable and diligent efforts of our people, the educational and economic condition of the Diaspora people is good. However, man cannot live by bread alone. Nor can life have meaning and value only through worldly pleasures. The words of the Bible are true always: *Is not life more than food and the body more than clothing?* (Matthew 6:25). If our church is not strengthened in its spirituality and in her apostolic mission, if the church does not go beyond the narrow mission defined by the community, and does not provide strong guidance in its message of Christian salvation, the younger generation in particular can quite easily seek that sustenance in other places—other Christian denominations or they can remain indifferent and become alienated from the Christian faith. . . .

Throughout the duration of the life of any Christian, he or she remains a child or child-like. That is to say, a Christian is always a student. Childhood is not only a matter of age, just as learning is not only a matter of the school term or year. Education is an indispensable part of our everyday life. In the same way, learning the Christian faith is not a matter of a desk or classroom. . . . Everything is changeable in this world, except the breath of God and His mark is within all of us. Those who seek it will find it. Christ said, *the sky and country will end, but my words will never end.*
Pastoral Letter, uncirculated, 1999.

Visit to Australia.

The strengthening of the Kevorkian Seminary was a priority for His Holiness. The Seminary was renovated, new dean and faculty members appointed, and qualified seminarians sought. His Holiness taught at the seminary on a regular basis.

The experience of suffering that we have lived through could not have happened without marking our mentality, our national being. In the Armenian culture, we have certain imprints left by that suffering, of which the most evident might be the melancholy that has affected our music and literature, so rich with elegies and lamentations.

But there is also the flip side of the coin. That suffering has actually created in Armenians the attitude that we must react, which has nothing to do with resignation or passivity, and which you could characterize as tenacity, perseverance, endurance. That is one of the traits of our character: a quality resulting from what we have experienced in life, which makes me think of Saint Paul's words to the Romans: *We celebrate even in our suffering because we know that suffering produces patience, patience produces resistance, and resistance produces hope*, (Rom. 5:3-4).

The sufferings of history were a test for the Armenians, a sort of challenge, to which they reacted not only by *enduring* that suffering, but also by *transcending* it through surprising creativity....

Often, suffering has been seen by historians, Armenian or not, as such a dominant aspect of our history that the very name Armenia is inseparably associated with suffering. The theologian and liturgist Archdale King said: *The historiography of Armenia is a synonym for martyrology*. While speaking of our martyrs in his history of the Church, the French academic Daniel-Rops uses the expression, *bleeding Armenia*, but adds subsequently the adjective *living*. I think that those two adjectives together offer a good definition: suffering has given our people the spirit to not resign themselves to death—to their disappearance. Thus, as paradoxical as it may seem, suffering has contributed to the development of the creativity of our people.

That is why, in going back to our literature, next to the numerous elegies to which I alluded, one of the major literary genres is the epic, which celebrates heroism.

Between Heaven and Earth, 1999

His Holiness Karekin I and His Holiness Aram I and clergy pray at the eternal flame in Dzizernagapert.

With the leadership of Karabagh at the dedication of a monument in honor of Monte Melkonian, May 1995.

*A*ncient churches, which until recent times were conceived and described as ancient national monuments, should be repaired and restored for use by the Church. They are magnificent pieces of architecture. But they should be given the breath of life. How would we feel if these famous historic Churches, the centers of our Armenian spiritual, educational and cultural life remain in their present-day state of ruined monuments and shown to our own young generation and to the world at large on the occasion of the 1700th anniversary? It is a pity if Datev and Noravank, Haghpat and Sanahin, Hardjavank and Marmashen, Hovhannavank and Saghmosavank, Khor Virap and Buragan, St. Garabed and St. Apostles, Moughni and Marian, and ancient churches in Yerevan Capital City remain until 2001 what they are today.... We need to find benefactors for the sponsorship of such renovation projects of paramount importance and of urgent need for restoration.
Under the Imperative of Renewal, 1998

*H*undreds of churches were closed in the last seven decades. Some were completely destroyed. Others were turned into buildings of secular public function. Still others stand there, in their place, damaged or in ruins....

The new Independent State of Armenia is ready to render back to our Church authority all such churches or monastic buildings. Our Church is ready to receive and transform them into active churches.... Several of them are already rendered back and some of them are renovated and already in actual use....

Besides the renovation of old churches we also face the need to construct new ones. In the last decades new towns have grown where there were no historic churches. New ones have to be erected to enable people to rally around and build their community life.
Etchmiadzin is Mission, 1996

A sentimental visit to the Monastery of Kanzasar.

*O*ur lives as clergymen—imbued by prayer and irradiated by dedicated and sacrificial work—is the most effective factor for the credibility and acceptability of Christ by the people. The preaching of the Gospel stems from life—from Christ's life—and passes through our lives, to be transmitted into the life of the people. "To do and to teach:" this is the true Christian model for preaching the Gospel, and for the vitalization of Christian faith in our daily lives. Our model, as servants of Christ, cannot be any other....

By the witness of history, we believe also that the general and dominant model set by our Holy Fathers was the same. Otherwise, for our nation, Christianity would not have been a living faith, which filled and directed the whole pattern and the peace of the life of Armenians during the last two thousand years. Without this existential dimension of the Christian faith, the continuous creativity of the Armenian nation—in the face of constantly threatened lives—would have been impossible and inexplicable.

As clergymen, will we be able to stand before the people of God, with clear consciences, and honestly say: "Whoever sees us, sees Christ"? The true definition of our identity and merit is prayer (as individuals and as a community), communion with God, and work dedicated to the people—this latter being a natural radiance of the first. The clergyman, through prayer and work, is the bridge that carries the faithful.

Inaugural Encyclical, 1995

*I*t is true that our State of Armenia through its Ministry of Social Affairs and other related agencies has integrated the social welfare service within its responsibilities. It is true that philanthropic or humanitarian organizations, national and international levels, such as the Red Cross and others are carrying on their mandate of social humanitarian services. But the Church as such cannot remain indifferent to this dimension of its Christ-given mandate and therefore is called to offer its share in this great task of what is usually described as *diaconal* calling.

The Church could not be actively engaged in such service in the time of Soviet rule over Armenia. After the emancipation from such a regime and in this new era of freedom and independence the Church has to resume its responsibilities in this respect.

His Holiness and clergy in the somber duty of the re-interment of the remains of the martyred Catholicos Khoren Mouratbegian.

Welcoming Lady Caroline Cox to Holy Etchmiadzin.

Seven years ago Armenia was shaken by the earthquake. The nation and the Church had to remedy the disaster that fell upon our country. We will always and forever be grateful to all the peoples, nations, states, churches, religions, humanitarian organizations, both national and international, ecumenical bodies such as the World Council of Churches and other international religious, Christian agencies for social assistance, Orthodox, Catholic, Protestant alike, who expressed their solidarity in an exemplary manner.

Our Church, through its spiritual center, the Mother See of Holy Etchmiadzin was extensively supported by the sister churches and ecumenical bodies and was fully engaged in relief and emergency service. Today it faces the challenge of social service as a *permanent* part of its task and mission....

The work in this area of service is supported to a considerable extent by various Armenian dioceses and philanthropic organizations from the Diaspora. The Mother See of Holy Etchmiadzin acts as a center of co-ordination and general supervision. I must say that already, through the help provided by the WCC and through the services of Hayastan Pan Armenian Fund we were able to establish a hospital for infectious diseases in Stepanakert in Nagorno Karabagh.....

Construction work for houses, which started soon after the earthquake, has now become part also of our Church center in the Holy See of Etchmiadzin. Certain projects are now in process in the earthquake zone, with the help provided by the WCC and the Fund for Armenian Relief of the Eastern Diocese of the United States....

What I would like to say in general terms is that the diaconal service of our Catholicosate of Etchmiadzin is geared into the direction of contributing towards the process of our people's becoming more and more self-reliant. And I personally and very strongly believe that the national health of our country lies in this kind of self-understanding and self-realization. All assistance from outside should promote this line of action. I emphasize this point because I realized in the last year of my ministry as Catholicos of All Armenians that the earthquake calamity, the conflict in Nagorno-Karabagh, the blockade imposed on our country for political reasons, the economic conditions of our country at this time of coming out of the Soviet economic system and entering into a new system of free economy, all these

Russian Patriarch Alexy II visits Holy Etchmiadzin.

The Romanian Patriarch visits Holy Etchmiadzin.

have contributed towards the sense of dependency. I observe the emergence of what I call an attitude of expectancy—looking forward to the outside world both to the Armenian Diaspora and non-Armenian sources for assistance.... We as a Church have to contribute towards this process of encouraging our people to become less and less dependent to outside help and more and more self-dependent. That is, so to say, to affirm our philosophy of diaconal service.
Etchmiadzin is Mission, 1996

Russian Christian history clearly reveals and amply proves the fact that the Christian faith penetrates in the whole texture of a nation's life molding the spirit of that nation and shaping the cultural, educational, moral and social components of their national life.

Your saints, monks, church divines, intellectuals, pastors, patriarchs, metropolitans, bishops, priests, played a determining role in the formation of your national identity and character. Who can study and truly understand Russian history without seeing the transfiguring power of the Christian faith as made manifest in and through the mystical elevations of your saints, the prayerful life of your monks, the cultural and artistic creations of your Church divines, the pastoral dedication of your bishops and pastors and the patriotic attachment of your people to your country through their great moral ideals and Christian principles of the Gospel?

The same trend of life and service has, indeed, been the typical way of Christian witness of the Armenian Church as is well known and recognized by all students of Christian and Armenian history....

This national character in both cases has never been an obstacle to the openness of both the Russian and the Armenian churches to other churches and cultures in the world. Your links with Byzantine, Slavonic and, later, with Latin Western cultures have been a source of ecumenical enrichment of the Russian Orthodox Church. In our Armenian experience, we also have been enriched with our openness to the early Christian patristic living tradition and to the Syrian, Greek-Byzantine and Latin Western Christian witnesses and cultural achievements.

Message to Patriarch of Moscow and of All Russias

Above: Welcoming the U.S. Ambassador, Peter Tomsen to Armenia.

Right: His Holiness in visit with the President of Italy, December 1996.

I come to you from the Mother See of our Armenian Church, the Catholicosate of All Armenians, Holy Etchmiadzin... I bring to Your Holiness and to the great Roman Catholic Church spread all over the world the seventeen centuries of faithful Christian witness symbolized by Holy Etchmiadzin, the birthplace and the baptismal font of our Armenian nation as a Christian nation. Let us together in all humility, render thanks and glory to the Holy Trinity, the Father, the Son and the Holy Spirit for this great miracle of retransfiguration that the historic land of Armenia experienced once more in its long, and often hardest, journey of pilgrimage in worship of Triune God and in service to humankind in the easternmost region of Asia Minor and the Caucasus.

We are approaching the end of the second millennium of Christian history. We are preparing to enter the third millennium. The world today is facing so many and so disturbing problems of mutual concern. I wholeheartedly welcome your enlightened advocacy for the revalorization of the spiritual values in a world affected by an extremely desacralized and secularized philosophy of life and culture. Moral principles of life embodied in the Holy Scriptures and in the tradition of the church are being trodden down in the name of such a pace of life which is depicted by the word of modernism and which is conceived as a new idol so heavily incensed in so many quarters around the world. Obviously, progress is an integral part of our Christian faith and life as designed by God. But progress is divinely genuine and humanly authentic in as much as it incorporates human values, spiritual and moral, intellectual and cultural in service to true happiness of men and women....

With these thoughts in mind and this desire in heart and this spirit in the soul, and as we pass through the blessed season of Advent in preparation for the celebration of our Lord's incarnation, I look forward to a brighter future wishing Your Holiness good health and ever-increasing bountiful ministry so essential and beneficial to all humankind and so faithful to our heavenly Father, His Only Begotten Son and the Holy Spirit.
Addressing Pope John Paul II, 1996

Karekin I at the Vatican with Pope John Paul II. 1996.

Six full weeks—from January 10 to February 20—I spent with you. I prayed with you, I spoke to you, opening widely my heart and mind to you. I listened to you, particularly through the voice of your younger generation. In one word, I communicated with you, sharing with you like bread, salt and water the living presence of God, of our Holy Church, of our Nation, and of our Homeland.
…I met with you, I witnessed to the revival of your faith; in all these experiences I felt uplifted and delighted by becoming more closely aware of your genuine love and dignified reception, which you so graciously showed towards the Catholicosate of All Armenians and the Mother See of Holy Etchmiadzin….

The reality of a spiritual re-awakening in the world of today is one of the most characteristic and eloquent phenomena of the present age, observable on a worldwide scale. Our nation cannot be but part of this movement. In the twilight of the second millennium of Christian history while all the churches and Christian nations are preparing to celebrate this significant milestone in the 2000-year life of Christianity, we Armenians will mark the 1700th anniversary of the recognition of Christianity as our state and national religion….

A visit with President Bill Clinton in the Oval Office, June 1998, when His Holiness came to the United States to preside over the Centennial Celebration of the Armenian Church in America.

His Holiness Karekin I during his visit to the United States with Alex Manoogian, right, and Kevork Hovnanian, left. Mr. and Mrs. Hovnanian were the sponsors of the renovation of the Kevorkian Seminary and Mr. Manoogian was the principle sponsor of the St. Gregory Cathedral in Yerevan.

It was an occasion of joy for me to witness among the faithful of your dioceses an exemplary attachment and a spirit of participatory contribution to the church, which were made manifest and were enhanced in the course of our pontifical visit.

I want to make a special appeal first to the clergy, to all the ministers of the Church....

My beloved brothers, dedicate yourselves with all your hearts, with all your minds, with all your energy, and through continuous, harmonious activities, with complete devotion and unselfish love to your Christ-given mandate of service; utilize to the highest degree your skills, time and resources; preserve faithfully the essential traditions of our holy church, cultivate the spiritual life of our people, and thereby make your God-given calling worthy to its Giver and productive for the benefit of His people. This is our foremost obligation as clergymen....

I appeal to all of our lay people, to the responsible people involved in church organizations, and to the individual faithful, that they regard the Church as their own home and behave accordingly, by offering their very best to her, so that they may remain spiritually healthy and morally strong, with a life enriched by happiness and fruitful with God-pleasing deeds....

With United Nations Secretary General Kofi Annan, June 1998.

Ecumenical visitors join His Holiness in a pilgrimage to Dzizernagapert, the Martyrs' Monument

In the course of my pontifical visit I noticed with great contentment that in all segments of our community a desire was developing for mutual rapprochement, in order to bring to an end the decades-long administrative division in the bosom of our church throughout the United States. I had the joy of coming into contact with the entirety of the faithful of our Church without discrimination. Among the clergymen and laymen greeting me I welcomed the presence of the church leaders and faithful who have been under the spiritual care of the Catholicosate of the Great House of Cilicia for the past four decades. Both in the United States and Canada, I paid visits to a number of churches affiliated with the Cilician See, which accorded me warm welcome. I learned that the doors of cooperation have widened during the recent years. I cannot forget especially the growing desire of the younger generation to put an end to the unnatural situation of our Church in the United States, and to rally around one Church under the jurisdiction of the Catholicosate of All Armenians....

Today, all the possibilities exist to create that normal situation. It remains to put it into effect, with a courageous stand, a broadminded approach and with the principle of mutual confidence.

Above: Sharing the joy under a huge tent in Ellis Island with Rudolph Giuliani, Mayor of New York, and His Eminence Archbishop Khajag Barsamian, Primate of the Eastern Diocese.

Right: A special visit to St. Nersess Seminary in New York.

During the whole duration of my visit and in my public utterances as Catholicos of All Armenians addressed to our people, I often and strongly expressed my paternal love and pontifical care for all the children of the Armenian Apostolic Church. I showed my willingness to administer the spiritual care of the Mother See of Holy Etchmiadzin to all, without discrimination. ...

One of the most brilliant and gratifying aspects of my first pontifical visit was that I witnessed the beautiful and hopeful phenomenon of re-awakened life and engagement of your new generation. You had proclaimed 1996 as "The Year of the Youth." My pontifical visit coincided with the beginning of that year. As spiritual father I rejoiced inwardly to have meetings with the members of the younger generation in every city and region. I heard their voice, and learned about the issues that concern and trouble them... It is my fervent desire and exhortation that the youth be given the opportunity to take a role in the responsible bodies of our Church. One of the most effective ways to positively shape the character of the youth is to place confidence in them, and as evidence of that confidence, to charge them with responsibilities. ...

*Visiting a long-time friend, John Cardinal O'Connor
in New York during His Holiness's pontifical visit to the Eastern Diocese.
With him is His Eminence Archbishop Khajag Barsamian.*

Throughout the expanse of the United States and Canada, you do your very best to be loyal and creative citizens, true to the highest ideals of your countries; and as such you have won honor and respect on the part of your fellow citizens, government officials and public leaders. Continue your course, because it constitutes the genuine expression of the authentic character of the Armenian people.

Alongside with all this, your ancestral land, the soil of your roots, your Mother Armenia, is present in your hearts and minds, indeed, in the whole ethos of your existence. In the United States and Canada, you know full well that there are people with different religious persuasions and ethnic origins, who keep alive their own traditions, thereby maintaining their harmony within diversity. This human mosaic is the strength and richness of your countries.

You bring into this context the color and voice of the Armenian people: our character at its best, our best-seeking and creative trend of life, and our spirit of enterprise. Even as you blend those distinct qualities and services into the systematic mix of society in America, you reserve a special place for your love and dedication towards your Armenian heritage and homeland.

A hearty welcome by Archbishop Iakovos, Primate of the Greek Orthodox Church.

Dr. Vartan Gregorian greets His Holiness and guests to Providence, Rhode Island, during the Catholicos's pontifical visit to the Eastern Diocese.

Your ancestral land, Armenia, has embarked on a new and luminous path.... The determining first five years of our new Republic proved to be a time of self-strengthening and restructuring. Let us kneel and offer praise to God that we are moving forward on this new path, in spite of all kinds and forms of crises...

Let the link between the homeland and the diaspora be strengthened on the basis of mutual love and confidence. Let us rise above the narrow mentality of local, partisan or individual interests, and frivolous, unimportant matters to which they divert our attention. Let us comprehend the real situation; make a comprehensive appraisal of issues and needs; appreciate whatever positive acts are accomplished, guided by a sense of good faith; indicate the shortcoming through a constructive criticism whose purpose is to correct the defects and wrongs. This is an attitude truly befitting Armenians both in the homeland and the diaspora. Let us not be victims of history, living only by the dictates of the past. Let us be makers of history, improving the present and putting the future on a firm foundation.

Thanks and Appreciation to the Diocese of
the Armenian Church of America, 1996
First Pontifical visit to the United States

Greeting the faithful in Boston.

I would like just to remind all of us…at the end of the 19th century, right after the massacres of Mush, Taron, and Sasoon, a prophetic figure like Khirmian Hayrig got the vision of establishing for the spiritual well being of his people, the Diocese in America. Our fathers came here as refugees, we should never, never forget that we came here escaping from death, agony, and tragedy. We found in this land a new life; the greatest virtue of that life being freedom, in which we could give expression to our own being as human beings with the Armenian color and experience in this country of America. Therefore in all humility I kneel before God together with you at this moment and render tribute to the everlasting memory of all my predecessors beginning from Khrimian Hayrig who established this Diocese up to my immediate predecessor, His Holiness Vazken the First of blessed memory, who surveyed and carried on the fartherly care for the Armenian community of America. I render homage to the everlasting memory of all those…who assumed responsibility in the running of the life of the Church, who had the courage to assume public responsibility…and who now are not on this earth but from their heavenly abode they rejoice because God gives them the bliss of internal peace….

Greeting the faithful in Florida.

Who are we today? Our country one hundred years ago was a valley of sorrow and death, people were receiving the news of massacres, persecution, genocide. Today there is the new light, the sun is shining forth in our motherland of Armenia. I am not coming to you from a country that mourns its dead but from a country that looks forward to becoming a worthy member of the world family of nations…. How are we going to relate ourselves to this new challenge? It is not only a gift, it is not only something we have just received, but something we have to render back to God, like the parable of the talents in the Gospel….

In the United States of America, it was the church that kept us firm in our faith, faithful to our identity, kept us creative in our Christian dignity. Therefore let us be once more conscious that today we are not going to give up our spiritual moral standards and become victims of a society which has become such a society of consumerism that is becoming a second idol or second god….

…Let us look forward with commitment to pursue, to promote what our fathers did and what we have done until now as constructive participation in the life of the church.

His Holiness in New York in May 1998, with senior clergy of the Armenian Church, and a group of key donors to the Centennial Endowment Fund. Pictured are: (front row left right) Bishop Aris Shirvanian, Archbishop Hovnan Derderian, Dr. Haroutune Mekhjian, Mrs. Shoghag Hovanessian, Mrs. Shake Mekhjian, Mrs. Hasmig Hovnanian, Mr. Sarkis Gabrellian, Archbishop Khajag Barsamian, Mrs. Siran Gabrellian, His Holiness Karekin I, Mrs. Takouhy Soultanian, Mr. Sarkis Soultanian, Mrs. Sirvart Hovnanian, Mr. Kevork Hovnanian, Mrs. Virginia Dadourian, Mr. Alex Dadourian, Mrs. Jill Kassis, Mr. George Kassis, Archbishop Datev Karibian; (middle row left to right) Mr. Haig Didizian, Mrs. Elza Didizian, Mr. Jerier Demirjian, Mrs. Mary Demirjian, Archbishop Karekin Nercessian, Ms. Manoushag Mathevosian, Mr. Harold Gulamerian, Ms. Anoush Mathevosian, Mrs. Josephine Gulamerian, Mrs. Margrit Atinizian, Mrs. Sonig Kradjian, Mr. Kegham Kradjian, Mr. Haig Tutak, Mrs. Vartouhi Tutak, Mrs. Astrid Dadourian, Mr. Haig Dadourian, Mr. Richard Dabagian, Mrs. Lucy Dabagian, Mrs. Edna Keleshian, Mr. Harry Keleshian; (back row left to right) Mr. Vahakn Hovnanian, Dr. Garo Garibian, Mr. Nishan Atinizian, Dr. Raffi Hovanessian, Mr. Michael Haratunian, Mrs. Marie Haratunian, Mr. Charles Pinajian, Mrs. Grace Pinajian, Mrs. Ica Kouyoumdjian, Mr. Hagop Kouyoumdjian, Mrs. Ani Beudjekian, Mr. Ohannes Beudjekian, Mrs. Ann Korian, Mr. Paul Korian, Mrs. Mariam Tatosian, Mr. Ed Gulbenkian, Mr. Mardiros Tatosian, Mrs. Jaklin Atinizian, Mr. Kevork Atinizian.

If tomorrow will not be better then today, then what is the meaning of our Lord who tells us to look forward, look upward and God will show you the way. Are we ready to look forward and look upward?....

Let us make this centenary of the Diocese of America a moment of renewal. The past does not need our prayers. The past belongs to God. What we are called for is to witness today in the present situation of our nation both in the motherland of Armenia and in the whole Diaspora. To witness to God, to witness to our history, to witness to humankind, and here you, with this centenary, to witness to the United States what you are, what you have been made in the image of God with the imprint of seventeen hundred years of Christian Armenian history.

To all of the Armenian community, without any kind of distinction, jurisdictional, political, social, or whatever else we human beings have created, I call upon with an invitation to a new centenary of renaissance. There is no distinction, no discrimination in the eyes of God. From East to West, from North to South, let all Armenian people, the Armenian American people, become in the coming century much greater than they have become up to the end of the first century.

Hrashapar Message, 1998
Celebrating the first century of
the Armenian Church in the United States

*His Holiness honor Mr. Jivan Gopoian
who sponsored the St. Mesrob Center in Oshagan.
The center is home to scholars as well as lectures and symposia. 1996.*

His Holiness with the President of Greece, Constantine Stefanopules, 1999.

My family was a very safe environment. We didn't know any particularly difficult times. From the material point of view, it was difficult; we never lived with abundance. But my father worked hard, and my mother did all that she could so that we wouldn't lack anything; she loved us so much that she made up for anything we lacked materially. Then there were our grandparents, uncles and aunts, cousins… It was a patriarchal family. We got together often; we all lived in the same neighborhood. The immediate family was inscribed within the extended one. It was in that simple and safe environment that we grew up.

My father gave me a sense of dignity, of rectitude, of fidelity to moral principles and to the homeland. He was devoted to Armenia's independence movement; when I was still a teenager, he had participated in the struggle of liberation against the Turks. He was a model to us.

My mother was devoted to our family, to us. The affection she showed us and the care she took for our home were exemplary. Like her mother, she was very devout and every day she would send us to church in the morning and in the evening. She taught me kindness and magnanimity, the attitude of never thinking ill of others….

….

I was so busy with my duties that I could rarely see them. So for many years, my mother suffered because of my absence. Presently, they still live in Canada; my father passed away fifteen years ago. My mother spends half the year with me; after so many years, I see that she is still the same person, the one that raised me when I was a child. Moreover, she has continued to treat me the same way. She even remakes my bed….

…She recognizes that I have duties, and in some way she's proud of it, saying that God has blessed her in me… But I will always be her child. When I work a lot, she worries; she's happy when I rest; when I am gone, she is not happy….

Between Heaven and Earth, 1999

Vehapar's family visited him shortly after his enthronement. Seated, left to right, Sona Sarkissian, Zohrab Sarkissian, His Holiness, Diramayr Ovsanna Sarkissian, Yester Sarkissian. Standing are his nephew and niece, Hagop and Taline.

In later years mother and son grew closer. Diramayr Ovsanna enjoyed her prolonged visits to Armenia. Here they are on the balcony of the Veharan in Etchmiadzin.

I can only give thanks and glory to God, for having enabled His Armenia flock to recover so quickly and to launch a new effort of outreach. I have personally felt the breath of renewal that has penetrated our people, particularly the youth. I see His hand at work in Armenia's spiritual renaissance.
The Ecumenical Challenge in Eastern Europe, 1998

KAREKIN II
Catholicos of the Great House of Cilicia

*T*his is the fourth time that I kneel on this sacred altar and commit myself to the service of God and my people. This is the fourth time that the words of Jesus, first addressed to Peter the Apostle, "Lovest thou me?" echo in my ears and in my heart.

It was just twenty-eight years ago, on this very same day of the 29th of May, the feast of Pentecost that I first knelt on this altar and was ordained a deacon. Three years later, I heard the same voice of Jesus and I answered His call by entering the priestly order on this very same altar. Twelve years passed and the same challenging voice of Jesus touched my ears. And again I stood ready before God, and said: "Thou knowest that I love Thee." I heard His command and His commission: "Feed my sheep." Thirteen years have gone by since that day when I was consecrated Bishop.

Today, at this solemn moment, when we are all reminded of the descent of the Holy Spirit through the Feast of Pentecost, the same voice again touches my ears: "Simon, son of John, lovest thou me?"

...

*T*oday, in the presence of God's spirit in this Cathedral, I humbly open my heart and mind to His divine guidance. I feel there can be no greater glory for a human being than being an instrument in the invisible and omnipotent hands of the Creator and a servant to the servants of the Lord and of His people.

I am particularly encouraged as I realize that I will greatly benefit from the rich experience and wisdom of His Holiness Catholicos Khoren I. He has devoted his forty years of service in the Church ministry to the enhancement of our community life. His most memorable achievements will pave my way and will provide me with an inextinguishable source of spiritual motivation and direction...

During the last six years I served my church outside of Lebanon, and because my ecumenical responsibilities took me to all parts of the world, I became even more deeply aware of the great importance of the historic role and mission of Lebanon: to serve mankind as a country of freedom, human dignity, and harmony. This centuries-old tradition should not be threatened because of the recent crisis. Hatred should vanish, for hatred

is only a power of destruction. Mutual love and respect should prevail....

I am encouraged by the spiritual support of my brethren, the religious leaders of this country and in the world. I depend so much on their constant prayers and spiritual fellowship. I think in this era of ecumenical encounter we all are mutually helped and enriched. We have to manifest our oneness and togetherness in order to be that catalyst for love, peace, and justice that the world needs and expects from all religions and their servants.

I am also encouraged with the new spirit of mutual love and respect that has dawned upon our own Armenian Church and people. The participation of the Holy See of the Catholicosate of All Armenians in Etchmiadzin in my election and consecration has filled my heart with joy and hope. I look forward to continuing and strengthening the brotherly relations of the Catholicosate of Etchmiadzin. It is my sincere hope that the misunderstandings and divergences, which are all of jurisdictional nature, will disappear motivated by the spirit of and concern for one church....

It is my sincere wish that under God's guidance our Catholicosate of the Great House of Cilicia will continue to become a real center and source of spiritual, educational and cultural achievements for the benefit of our people.... Through renewed efforts focused on the seminary, we hope new and younger clergymen and lay leaders may be trained and well prepared to meet the needs of our people.

The second immediate area of concern should be the integration of our young generation, both men and women, in the whole process of our community life in all its various aspects. The young people should be participants in the process of both planning and implementation of such projects and activities that are aimed at the renewal of our community life....

I commit myself to the hands of the Lord and I enter the field with faith, hope, and love.

The Imperative of Love, 1977
Sermon delivered at consecration as Catholicos-Coadjutor of
The Great House of Cilicia

Catholicos Khoren I anoints the head of Catholicos-Coadjutor Karekin II, May 1977.

We have a small piece of land, which is fully occupied by Armenians, that is, Soviet Armenia, where we have about three million Armenians living on that small piece of land of our historical motherland. And then we have the dispersion within the Soviet Union, outside of Soviet Armenia, and we have also the dispersion outside the Soviet Union. We have Armenian communities in almost every country in the world that you can travel. Even when I went to New Zealand, for the executive committee of the World Council of Churches, I met Armenians. In Australia, in Calcutta, in Canada, in Europe, in the Middle East, we have small or larger communities continuing their national, religious, cultural, and linguistic heritage....

The church is a national church, It has become so much integrated in the national life of our history, that whatever we have—a sacred tradition inherited from the past—is embodied in that Christian tradition in our church. The church is the rallying point. The church is the focus of our community life wherever we go. That is why in so many communities the first thing when Armenians get together is to build a church. And next is to build a school—to preserve the language. In some countries, I know, to preserve the language is difficult. That sense of belonging to a national ethos which is embodied in the church, when particularly the nation is deprived of an independent state is what keeps us together. It is the golden thread, the church, all through the communities in the Diaspora and relating them also to the Motherland.

...The Catholicos is chief of the bishops. In other words, he is the first among equals. He is elected by the representatives of all the dioceses under the jurisdiction of the Catholicosate. The Catholicos in our church symbolizes the unity of the church and, also, in a sense, being the head of the nation as far, as long, as we don't have a king, or a president, or an independent state....

...I have served...our community in the United States... and I have a very special attachment to our people in the United States.... The major problem in my understanding is that the relationship of our Christian faith as transmitted to us by Christ through the Gospel and handed down to us through the tradition of our fathers, has to be communicated to the young generation in a meaningful and relevant manner. We have a new generation born in the United States of America. They don't

The courtyard of the Cilician Catholicate as the newly consecrated Karekin II leaves the Cathedral.

speak Armenian as fluently as we do here in the Middle East, but they are very conscious of their Christian and national heritage. Therefore, they have to be given the full knowledge of what is embodied in this centuries old Christian tradition. But, not in an archaic sense. That is, not looking back to history, but it should be a kind of relationship of that faith relating to the life of the people living today in a particular condition of life in the United States. Unless we bring that faith into the context of the life of today—the modern age of our young generation—I think we will miss the train. That is to say, they will follow the church only nominally, if they ever do. Therefore, the primary task, the most important and urgent task of the church is to be not only a place of worship, but also, as I used to call it, a kind of school. A spiritual school in which the souls are built...in which that inner edification of people is done or achieved. We have a lovely saying in the eastern Christian orthodox tradition, "The church is that place where the human person is transfigured." Like on the mountain of Tabor—as we have it in the Gospel—when you are imbued with the presence of God and you live your life with that consciousness of God's presence in you, which is the source of happiness for all people in all parts of the world.

...

There is a new awareness, a sort of renewal of consciousness. For more than one reason. In the first place we have this ethnic consciousness emergence in the United States. I became very familiar with it because I saw it not only in my community, but also in the other communities. People are looking for their roots—and that word, you know, is a capturing word these days in the United States. People are looking into their being, as not being conditioned with the present only, but because we have certain conditionings in us that we have inherited from the past. Besides that, there has been a complete change of the image of the Armenians today. Some thirty, forty, fifty years ago the Armenians were looked upon as "starving Armenians." Those who survived the massacres, those who escaped, they came to the United States as refugees.... The image was not as bright then as it is today. But, in the last few decades a complete transformation has taken place—where a new generation, as I said, born in the States, educated in the States, can relate with any other person in the United States on the same level of equality. Therefore, they have developed in them a very strong sense of identity and dignity....

...

Karekin II in front of the Cathedral of St. Gregory the Illuminator, Antelias, Lebanon.

My first immediate concern [as Catholicos] is to devote all my energy and to have my colleagues, my associates, my bishops, my priests and lay people to devote their efforts towards the formation of a new young leadership in our church. Therefore, the first institution within the Catholicosate that is going to have my priority will be the Seminary—the education, theological training of our young students. And I would like to increase the number of students and also enhance the quality of teaching. Because it is man who cultivates the earth. Without men and women, life is of no meaning. It is a kind of blind existence. And in the church what can we do to promote the Christian principles of life, the Christian faith, the cultural activities without men that are well equipped to carry out that kind of task? Second, I would like to see the scope of action of this Catholicosate extend beyond the boundaries of Lebanon. In other words, the Catholicosate should be at the service, practical service, to our people within our jurisdiction.... Third, I believe that our young people in any part of the world, but particularly in the United States, constitute our hope. I was so happy to have known this generation...Confident in themselves, proud of their heritage, proud of their American citizenship and American life. All this potential has to be geared into the life of the church, the life of our community, the life of the perpetuation of our culture.
Interview with CBS television, 1977

This monument commemorating the Armenian Genocide of 1915 and symbolizing the rebirth of the Armenian nation was erected in Bikfaya, Lebanon, the site of the Monastery of the Cilician See, in 1970. Bishop Sarkissian was instrumental in every aspect of this project from the concept to the final realization.

The recent fighting in the Eastern quarters of the city of Beirut and the suburbs as well as in some parts of the mountain villages stated on Saturday, 30th September, at about 9 a.m. It continued until 2:30 p.m. I was in Antelias and could see the rockets falling on the seaside, some twenty meters away from the Catholicosate, our residence, as well as in the neighboring orange orchards and residential areas.... The sound was most terrifying. Small pieces of shrapnel were falling in the main courtyard of the Catholicosal residence.

At 6 p.m. when the fighting had subsided, I could leave Antelias and go to Bikfaya, the summer residence, eight miles away from Antelias up in the mountains.... There, together with His Holiness Catholicos Khoren I and the members of the Religious Brotherhood...we spent the evening being very much concerned.... The next day we celebrated the Liturgy in the Chapel of Bikfaya. Very few people attended; they feared that the shelling could be resumed at any moment. There was sporadic fighting in the afternoon.

That same night, or rather at 2:30 a.m. the next morning, we all got out of our beds. The whole building was shaking because of the heaviest bombardment that I had ever seen in my life. I ordered all the priests and some twelve Seminary students who were staying in the Seminary during the summer season, to walk downstairs and to take shelter in the ground floor behind the thick walls built with stone. The rockets were coming from almost all directions. We could not identify the places they were fired from. One fell at the entrance of the neighboring hotel, two hundred meters away from our residence and one just in our own vineyard, adjacent to the building.

That same morning...at 6 a.m., I left Bikfaya and came down to Antelias. The shelling was continuing without interruption. This was real war. During that whole week...East Beirut and the neighboring suburbs came under continuous fire. It was almost impossible to move out of our residence. Communications were completely broken off. I could see from the balcony of our residence looking over the sea thousands of cars passing in a frenzy through the highway, towards the North. People were fleeing from the dangerous zones and trying to find shelter outside the city.... About 300 of them came to the Catholicosate where we had to accommodate them in the Seminary building and the classrooms of the George Mardikian

His Holiness inspects the damage within the Catholicate's complex.

School. I was deeply distressed to see so many people bewildered and shaken.... [All of us] did our utmost to take care of the people sheltered in the Catholicosate for the next three weeks, by providing them food, medicine, and spiritual comfort....

During the time of the heaviest fighting, I sent one bishop and three priests to the district of Bourj-Hammoud, where we have the largest concentration of Armenians. Shells were still continuing to fall on that densely populated area.

At this latest round of fighting the Armenians suffered most because the strategic points of the war was the area of the two bridges linking Bourj-Hammoud and the city of Beirut. The Armenian quarters geographically were the closest area to the war-field.

Notes from a personal diary, 1978

Hardship and suffering have reached such dimensions that they have become an existential reality in our life, intimately interwoven in the texture of our existence in the last five years. Do we want to describe the crisis? Is there need for it? Is it possible? What to say without leaving many other things unsaid? Shall we speak of disorder, anarchy, insecurity, uncertainty, violence, kidnappings, looting, violations of human rights, extensive use of drugs, increasing worship of mammon, lack of a sense of public responsibility, exploitation and manipulation of men and women, snipers' shootings, indiscriminate shelling, what else! More than twelve plagues have fallen upon us; which one is to be discussed?

Let us be frank. We in Lebanon have suffered so much from the lack of sincerity, openness, straightforwardness, that quite a number of our problems today have emerged from failure in the art of true and genuine dialogue—dialogue with ourselves and dialogue with others.

Face to Face with Suffering, 1979

But in spite of all the calamities, anxieties, suffering, destruction and losses that our people were subjected to, I thank God for having looked upon us with His grace of love and divine care. Through His life-giving power of spiritual sustenance and hope we have been able to

A powerful car bomb inflicted further damage to the Catholicate.

continue our obedience to Him and our commitment to His Kingdom by trying to be at service to the people in need and distress. In fact, most of my time and energy in this past year was spent in making every effort humanly possible to alleviate the suffering, to offer spiritual nurture from His Word and the Sacraments of the Church.
Christmas Letter, 1979

Between the 11th and 14th centuries—the period of the Armenian Kingdom of Cilicia—an era of interchurch relations of the foremost importance and having an enriching value opened for the Armenian Church.

The fall of the Bagratid Kingdom (885-1045) and the emigration of the Armenians toward the western regions—with the encouragement of the Byzantine Empire—offered to the Armenian Church the opportunity of lasting contact with other churches. Most notable among these were the Greek Orthodox Church, the Syrian Orthodox Church, and the Latin Church. The geographical and political isolation of the mountains of Armenian Major was broken. The Armenian people now found itself in an environment in which association with the other Christians of the region and those of the West, especially through contact with the Crusades, became both necessary and vital.

It is for this reason that one can rightly consider this period of the Armenian Kingdom of Cilicia as the most ecumenical in Armenian history. It is comparable in spirit to the "Golden Age" (fifth century) when the writing, literature, liturgy, and thought of the Armenian Church took shape in lasting contact with the universal church, represented in the Orient by the two branches of the Christian tradition, the Byzantine and Syriac. In this sense one could extend the expression "Silver Age," which is generally used for the literature and the culture of the Armenians from the 12th to the 13th centuries, to the Church and its ecumenical witness. For the opening thus created does not limit itself simply to politics, demographics, and culture, but also touches the Church, which is so closely tied to the life and fate of the Armenian people.
Le Royaume Arménien de Cilicie, 1993

Above: His Holiness had the utmost of respect for scholars and intellectuals and was always pleased to be in their company. This photograph was taken in New York City during the four-day Symposium on the Kingdom of Cilicia which brought together scholars and specialists from around the world. 1993.

Right: Charles Aznavour was one of the first international stars to perform in war-torn Lebanon.

*B*ut this year, April 24 has a radically different, exceptionally special and supremely unique character for us. Every year Der Zor, the most dramatic spot of the massacres and the genocide, used to echo on the lips of the millions of our people in all parts of the world with a special tone of affliction and indignation. Continuous repetition through the years made it to become just a word, a memory, a name, a symbol. This year and on this very day, Der Zor is a concrete, visible, palpable and breathable reality and atmosphere, concrete sand and desert to which we have come to be mixed with it and be imbued by it with an existential experience of life and symbolic sensitivity.

Today, as the Catholicos of the centuries-old and now exiled Holy See of the Great House of Cilicia, I have come to visit you, beloved martyrs, to renew our covenant with you and to incense your relics in the sand of this desert, to anoint them with the oil of our love, as the women went to incense the body of their Heavenly Teacher, Jesus Christ, on the third day of His crucifixion in the garden where His tomb was heavily closed with a huge stone and vigilantly guarded by the Roman soldiers.

...

*A*t this moment, on this sacred soil of Der Zor, having focused upon your memory the luminous rays of highest tribute from your revived, vibrant, and creative nation from all corners of the earth, I now humbly proceed to lay this foundation stone of a church dedicated to your martyrdom, as a token of eternity, as a sign of resurrection, as an assurance of hope and as a signpost of vision.

The chapel and martyrs monument in Der Zor, where thousands upon thousands of Armenians perished during the forced deportation, was a special project spearheaded by the Catholicos. The consecration of the complex of buildings was witnessed by thousands of Armenians from around the world.

Arise, stand on your feet and look what I have brought to you as a gift for the 70th anniversary of your martyrdom: I have brought to you a handful of soil and a piece of rock from the fertile soil and solid stone of Mother Armenia, so that you may feel the warmth and the strength of your country and the sweetness of the life-giving breath of your fathers and their new descendants. Accept them as inexhaustible nurture from your people on their way to victory.

Arise, stand on your feet and look what I have brought to you as a gift for this 70th anniversary: I have brought to you a handful of soil from that piece of land in Antelias, where the centuries-old Catholicosate of the homeland of Cilicia was reborn and where it is now more than forty years that the relics of some of you are buried. There, in the chapel named after St. Stephen the Protomartyr, the first martyr of Christendom, every visitor comes as a pilgrim and is inspired by your spirit of sacrificial life expressed through your crucifixion. This handful of soil taken from their tomb, where the tears and prayers of your people have blessed it, I now mix in the foundation of this new Chapel of Martyrs as mortar of our love.

Words from the Living to the Dead, 1985

Martyrs' Day commemoration in Antelias, 1991.

... $\mathcal{T}$he days between the 3rd to the 12th of February that I spent in New York together with my spiritual brother, His Holiness Vazken I, Catholicos of All Armenians, jointly sponsoring the noble task of the participation of the Armenian communities in the United States and Canada…in the reconstruction of the cities, towns and villages destroyed by the tragic earthquake in the Leninakan area, especially of the town of Stepanavan, were most highly significant days in my life, and, I believe, in your own lives.

You are well aware of the spirit of mutual brotherly love, deepest unity and unreserved dedication in which we the two Catholicoi, together carried on our common mission during our stay in New York. We together tried to convey to all of you, our distinct feeling and understanding that our Church and Nation, both in our Motherland of Armenia and in the Diaspora, are passing through such crucial and decisive times that the togetherness of all those who confess the same faith, share in the same church tradition, carry in their veins the same blood, hold the same heritage, speak the same language, look to the same future, is of absolute importance and should be considered the highest priority in all our common action….

Looking back on the unique and unprecedented experience of our joint visit to New York, as I, in this monastic setting of our life here in Antelias, reflect upon all that happened during the ten days of our stay in New York. I render thanks to God who graced our lives with such days that surely will be remembered in history as one of the brightest pages of our annals, as an achievement which comforted and strengthened us after the trials of our people in Azerbaijan, because of the Karabagh issue, and particularly because of the deadly blow of the earthquake of December 7, 1988….

I earnestly pray that the same spirit of oneness and togetherness will prevail in the life of our communities in the United States. If you listen to the truly authentic voices of our history, if you are sensitive in perceiving the vision of our future, please line-up your lives and deeds of the present times in the direction of collaboration, common activities, joint ventures, unified actions giving concrete proof of your national unity and dignity.

A true friendship marked with respect and love developed between Karekin II and Vazken I. The earthquake in 1988 deepened the friendship as the two Catholicoses worked together to help the people of Armenia. This photograph was taken in February 1989 in New York City when the two pontiffs joined hands to mobilize the Diaspora.

In this year of 1989, as we will enter the last decade of the twentieth century, let us all make a special effort of "reading the signs of the time." The signs clearly indicate, as I mentioned in my last sermon at St. John the Divine Cathedral in New York... that the future is for true dialogue and convergence; dialogue not only in words but in life and in action. Our common cause needs us all and needs us all together. The sign and the cry, the pain and the suffering of our Motherland reach and touch us all; and they can be alleviated when they find us together.

We, Catholcos Vazken I and myself, committed ourselves together to this understanding. You saw us standing before God and you together, praying together, speaking together and working together....

I earnestly pray that our joint visit will prove an excellent opportunity and a productive stimulus of inner search of souls and of drawing closer together for all our people.... This is a time that calls for dedication through concerted efforts in response not only to the needs of reconstruction and redressment for our Motherland and people in Armenia, but also for the renewal and regeneration of our people in the Diaspora.

Pastoral Letter, 1989

I know well the extent to which that earthquake was a horrible calamity, an extremely difficult experience. I know how much suffering it caused, since I went to Leninakan, from Lebanon, ten days after the catastrophe. I saw with my own eyes the despair of the mothers looking for their children, the lines of coffins, the ruins, the piles of debris. At night, when I went back to Etchmiadzin, I was in a state of indescribable distress. But before that general destruction, I understood that we should not let ourselves be overcome with despair, that we had to react immediately to work on the reconstruction, which I said the next day in celebrating the Liturgy in the Cathedral of Holy Etchmiadzin. In this way, I found the strength to move on from that state of spiritual prostration.

I understood very well that when you lose a person who was dear to you, when you learn that someone has a fatal disease, you wonder why? But this question cannot be answered logically. There are many aspects of our lives that cannot be explained. When the clouds hide the sun, you don't really wonder why God

Visiting Datev Monastery in the Siunik region of Armenia with Catholicos Vazken I.

is making it so; it is something that is a part of nature, part of the rhythm of life. Faith reveals itself precisely when our logic does not understand.

So the question of why the earthquake happened, or illnesses, remains without a logical response for us; here, it is a matter of believing that God is present even at the lowest point of the test.

...

*T*here are two levels of meeting with God in the test, which I have experienced in my life and which I clearly noted after the earthquake of 1988.

The first level is complete distress, even revulsion. You wonder where God is; you have the impression that he is absent. Such is the reaction when you are facing general destruction as in Spitak. But immediately after the earthquake, the demonstrations of solidarity with an unheard of generosity began to emerge: food, medications, clothing and other forms of help arrived from everywhere. Many men and women from every country came to Armenia to help look for bodies and to help in the reconstruction. Such generosity allowed us all to feel God's presence. That solidarity was the manifestation of true humanity, which is the influence of God: Love.

I think that it often happens like that. In these tests, there is always a moment of crisis, a moment when one experiences the absence of God. It is a matter of going beyond that moment of doubt and solitude, that moment of abandonment, through an act of faith and love. That is how you see that God is present— that He was always beside us, that He was there even in His absence.

Between Heaven and Earth, 1999

*O*ur Church and Nation are called today to prove themselves to be one by becoming one concerted entity. Yes. Composed of different parts, yet, united in spirit, in purpose and in mutual understanding and collaborative policy and action....

This is, I believe, my dear friends, why we, the two Catholicoi of the Armenian Church, His Holiness Vazken I and myself, came together and did our best to give concrete

*The hierarchy of the Armenian Church:
Left to right, Patriarch of Jerusalem, His Beatitude Archbishop Torkom Manoogian;
His Holiness Vazken I, Catholicos of All Armenians; His Holiness Karekin II,
Catholicos of the Great House of Cilicia; and the Patriarch of Istanbul,
His Beatitude Archbishop Karekin Kazanjian, in Etchmiadzin.*

expression to that sacred unity. We are committed to continue to do so in the future. Never before in our history, since we have had the two Catholicosates, from 1441 on, has happened what in fact did happen in the past few years. In the last two years the two Catholicoi met four times, twice in Armenia our Motherland. I still deeply feel that spirit that I felt in Etchmiadzin, in Armenia: being together, standing side by side at the altar of the Mother Church in Etchmiadzin, walking in a joint march towards the monument of the Martyrs in Dzidzernakapert in our capital city of Yerevan, visiting together the whole region of the southeast of Armenia, the province of Siunik and the mountains of Zangezour close to Karabagh, and facing the people, opening up to them our hearts and minds and seeing them with eyes filled with joy and bright expectations in which one could easily read their faith, hope and love. I turned and said to Vehapar Vazken that in these moments it is not to this or that person, to this or that period of history that I feel our eyes are fixed upon, but upon the whole future of our Church and Nation.

...

Let me be as honest as humanly possible: In my assessment, the situation of today is not that crystal clear. After spending ten days together with His Holiness Catholicos Vazken I in Brussels and Paris on my way to the United States, after hours of personal discussions, I share his anxieties for the future of Armenia. I cannot perceive clearly at this stage what may happen in the whole of the Soviet Union. Surely, we recognize certain trends. We may analyze them, weigh their significance for the future; but we are not their masters. There are things happening beyond and above our will. What we must be doing, in my humble reckoning, is to be alert, to stand together, to closely watch the events with greater discernment than we have done before, and align our action accordingly and not be taken aback or be left without a choice of our own.

The Armenian Church Facing the 21st Century, 1990

Vazken I and Karekin II in front of the Cathedral of St. Gregory, Holy Etchmiadzin.

The last decades of the Kingdom of Cilicia were marked by a more profound penetration of latinophile leanings, especially in the circles of the nobility assembled around the royal court. The last kings, themselves of French origin (Lusignan) and belonging to the Roman Catholic Church, were the agents of this penetration and were thus the cause of the alienation of the people that contributed to the decline and, ultimately, fall of the state....

The openness of ecumenicity of the Armenian Kingdom of Cilicia expresses itself on the ecclesiastical plane as much as at the political, cultural, and social level.

Relations with the Latin Church, the most powerful church of the period, were pursued while being tied to political relations by the concern for security and protection on the part of the Armenian people and by the desire for power and expansion on the part of the Latin Church.

The relations between the two churches remained formal and touched only a class of the Armenian clergy and people in Cilicia, primarily in the capital of the kingdom and the circles associated with the royal court. They did not affect the people, the *laos*, the foundation of the composition of the church. These were, in the strict sense of the word, interecclesiastical relations rather than relations encompassing the *ecclesia*, the totality of the ecclesial reality.

It is clear that in the case of the Armenian Church it was the Cilician region that was engaged in these relations. The greater part of Armenia Major, the bishops, clergy, monasteries, and people of Armenia proper, lived not only uninvolved and unaffected but they went even further: they conducted a fierce opposition and created an entire movement of contestation and refusal.

...The Armenian Kingdom of Cilicia offered to the Armenian Church a new era of enrichment. Once more, the historical truth has been reaffirmed according to which the encounter between the churches, despite all the vicissitudes that they cross, proves itself enriching. This enrichment is more authentic when it is not contrary to the identity of a particular church, an identity which, for the cause of the unity of the church, must always be understood to be part of the common identity of Christ.

Le Royaume Arménien de Cilicie, 1993

Above: With President Mitterand of France at the opening of the exhibit devoted to the Armenian Kingdom of Cilicia, in Paris.

Right: Visiting Diocese of Kuwait and Arabian Gulf Countries: Left to right, Khatchig Babikian, His Holiness, His Excellency Dr. Sheikh Sultan Bin Mohammad Al-Kasimi, the Ruler of Sharjah, and Bishop Oshagan Choloyan. The Sheikh accepted His Holiness' request for permission to build a church in Sharjah, United Arab Emirates, and also donated the land. March, 1995.

... We had a feeling of gratitude toward the Arabs and a great respect for their culture, because since the time of the genocide they had welcomed us with open hearts. We knew their hospitality very well and we restarted our lives in the countries of the Near East thanks to that brotherhood of Arabs.

Between Heaven and Earth, 1999

The Diaspora has been a permanent aspect of Armenian life throughout history. After the First World War it became a most important factor in the whole life of the Armenian people and their church.

In the aftermath of the war, the situation of the Armenian people presented a picture of complete desolation. The people were migrating in all directions wherever they could find refuge: the Middle East, Europe (mainly France), the United States and South America. The first years were a period of settlement and adjustment. They lived now in new countries; they met new peoples; they began to speak new languages; they adopted new customs; they came in touch with new cultures. They had to find their way in a world-situation of most varied scope and character. Indeed, the recovery and revival of the Armenian Church in the Diaspora is amazing. A refugee people at the end of the First World War, the surviving Armenians soon rebuilt new homes in the countries which received them and which they considered as their second fatherland. They offered their wholehearted contribution to all peoples and countries with which they shared their new life.

The Armenian Church in Contemporary Times, 1969

His Holiness is showered with flowers by school students in Los Angeles, 1988.

There are problems yet unsolved; many areas of life are still in need of the vivifying power of the spirit of God. This family of churches is called to fully participate in the rhythm of human life particularly in the Middle East where the old and the new are being brought together in this crucial, decisive moment of Middle Eastern history. The growth of a synthesis between the old and the new is not easy to obtain. Conflicts, clashes, setbacks are to be reckoned as part of the struggle. This is a hard way to march in. And our peoples of the Middle East are already engaged in it through a struggle between tradition and modern demands for change. No nation or church can live without tradition. Yet, it is equally true that no nation or church can live with tradition alone.

The church is the witness to the truth that the new has its roots in the old and the old has no sense unless it is renewed. The Christian faith is old and new at the same time and renewing at all times. It transcends the limitations of time and space. Yet it is expressed by being constantly renewed for the life of men in time and space. Here lies the dilemma. Here is also the great challenge for the constant renewal of man.

The Witness of the Oriental Orthodox Churches, 1968

We must always remember that Lebanon became our home as an Armenian community particularly after the massacres of 1915; but we must not forget that there was an Armenian community in Lebanon long before the First World War. And when the Armenians came to Lebanon after the attempted genocide, they felt at home in Lebanon. Our Catholicosate of Cilicia, having been uprooted from Cilicia itself, from its original seat, after nine years of peregrination between Syria, Lebanon and Cyprus, finally chose Lebanon for its headquarters….

I greet in this hall, three generations.

First, the generation of the people who are in their advanced age, that of our fathers and mothers. I pay respect

With Governor and Mrs. George Deukmejian in California. 1983.

to them for having done what they have done for us, the second generation. Those who are born in the Diaspora, you here in the United States of America, I in Syria or another one in Lebanon or in Iran or other parts of the Diaspora, who are educated in the Diaspora and received through that education, the sense of self-reliance which our fathers lacked because of their sense of inferiority when they came out of their ancestral country and could not speak the languages of the countries they settled in.... It was not easy for them to adjust themselves.... Their motto was how to survive, and how to educate their children. Our poet, Hovhannes Toumanian, has a few lines that are eloquent in this respect: "Live children, but do not live like us." That is their message to us.

The second generation has now upon its shoulders the responsibility of our community life around the world. History will tell what we do with that responsibility.

Hask, 1983

Fifty years, after all, is not a long period of human history. The Catholicosate of Cilicia, in its last 50 years in Antelias, particularly through its seminary, has provided the Armenian nation all over the world with three Catholicoi: Zareh, of ever-blessed memory; Khoren, a citizen of heaven; and myself, still militant for God on this earth. Also, 24 archbishops and bishops, 58 *vartabeds* [celibate priests], 105 *kahanas* [married priests], 216 teachers. Isn't this a contribution to our nation? Antelias has done this without any kind of jurisdictional discrimination. Today in France there are eleven celibate priests from the rank of bishop to the local parish level priests—eleven out of 22 who are graduates of our seminary

With the General Secretary of the United Nations, Javier Perez de Cuellar, 1983, in U.N. headquarters, New York City.

With Senator Charles Percy. 1983.

serving the one church under the jurisdiction of Etchmiadzin.

. . . . Never, never from my lips has there been any word said against Etchmiadzin or bringing Etchmiadzin under any kind of shadow, because I believe that Etchmiadzin is the very heart of our church as Armenia is the very heart of our existence, and whoever cuts himself or herself from that reality, that central reality of our being, does damage to his or her own existence. My feeling is as deep as that.

. . . .

My message today—if there were a single message—would be the following: We have enough enemies around us. Let us not become enemies with one another. People, organizations, states around the world seeing this renaissance of our people are being disconcerted. There was mention of the case of Cyprus. I have been one of those church leaders who, together with the head of the church in Cyprus and the church in Greece, who have done whatever we could to bring to world attention this great injustice committed before our own eyes on the island of Cyprus.

What counts is what you do. What counts is not what you think, what you feel; that is good but that is not good enough. History is not made of those things that people have thrown in the air, but of things tangible that have been materialized and have become a source of goodness and benefit to others.

A Pontifical Journey, 1983

Above: With Senator Robert Dole and Archbishop Mesrob Ashjian, Prelate of the Eastern Prelacy, in Washington, D.C., 1983.

Right: With the Speaker of the House of Representatives, Tip O'Neill, and the Chaplain of the House.

... **W**e as a church have to be concerned about the future of this nation. All churches in the world are concerned with the problems of human society. When there is apartheid in South Africa, all the churches speak against it. I am not ashamed as an Armenian churchman to speak against those injustices that have been committed to our nation. It is my Christian and national obligation to speak about it and to make the world aware to see that justice is done.... Recently I went to Der Zor, I saw the desert. I was travelling in a Cadillac, and I was having a very strong sense of guilt. I was seeing all of the desert, 600 kilometers, and I was imagining the tens and hundreds and thousands of my people being killed. Where is the world? And today, having said nothing, having only asked that justice be done, when people come and speak against this nation and say that there was no genocide, should we be silent? No. We have to come forward to speak in the churches, to speak in public, to public officials, and not to be taken for granted and go into oblivion.... Why should I be ashamed to tell the world that I cannot accept to be treated in the way my father was treated?

A Pontifical Journey, 1983

No church, which truly confesses her loyal dedication to the message and mission of the Incarnate Lord, can escape political responsibility. Particularly in this age of a "politicized" society, where political problems of both national and international scope confront all human endeavors, the churches' responsibility in international affairs has become more and more significant.

Cardinal John O'Connor, Archbishop of New York, in a visit to Antelias, Lebanon, in a show of solidarity, during the height of the Lebanese war.

Yet there is one aspect in this whole realm of the churches' concern for international affairs that needs further and deeper study. Where and how do we draw the line of distinction between the specifically political ways of solving political issues, and the political principles by which the churches deal with such issues? For it must be admitted that it is not so easy to resist the temptation of being involved in what is usually understood as *politics*, which obviously is not the task of the church as such.

The involvement of a church in the national life of her people is but natural. No church can really meet the soul of man in community without passing through the channels of national language, culture and, indeed, all the manifestations of the ethos of a nation. Christ Himself fully shared the life of His own people. Yet He transcended the conditions and aspirations of the Jewish people by seeing the whole Jewish tradition in the light of God's kingdom on earth, and by interpreting the whole meaning of Jewish history from the perspective of the universality of God's action in the world. Christ was never "caught up in politics," in spite of all temptations and traps. He had, so to speak, His own policy with its own principles and goals, which could not be conducted by the same rules and techniques as those of ordinary and conventional politics.

A Note on the Political Responsibility of the Churches, 1967

This Seminary is a center from where servants of peace, servants of God, servants of our people, will come forward and will bear witness through their dedicated life and work to the spiritual values which make any country stand firm and radiant.... The construction of this building is a living and eloquent expression of our firm faith in

Above: The class of deacons at the Seminary with His Holiness Khoren I (third from left) and the Dean of the Seminary, Bishop Karekin Sarkissian (second from left), 1965.

Right: His Holiness greeting Professor Puzant Yeghiayan in 1983. Professor Yeghiayan was a teacher at the Cilician Theological Seminary for 40 years, from 1932 when the Seminary was established to his retirement in 1972.

Lebanon and in the eternal truth as embodied in the will of God, which is one and the same towards all peoples: peace, harmony, and good will.

So many Armenians in the Arab world, in the Middle East, in Europe and in North America look to this institution as a center of formation of a young and dedicated leadership. Together with our assistants, both clerical and lay people, we will do our utmost to fulfill their aspirations and expectations.

Comments at opening of new Seminary building in Bikfaya, Lebanon, 1985

*A*s this exhibition makes clear, the production of books is, indeed, most impressive and highly commendable. However, the real value of the book is not in its sheer *production*, but in its *becoming available to the people*. In a deep sense, it is the reader that makes the book. Reading is the direct way of communicating with great minds and hearts.

The world of books and literature has been a familiar and cherished world in Armenian history. Tens of thousands of survived manuscripts bear eloquent witness to this historical truth.

But we don't live in history. We should continue that sacred legacy of our fathers today particularly in the Diaspora.

Today, the production of books has become a commercialized area of occupation. There are a great number of various kinds of books. One has to choose. The choice is indicative to the taste and desire for greater knowledge and sound judgement about values. We Armenians should never forget that literature began in our history with the Sacred Book, the Bible. There is a kind of sacredness attached to our literary heritage. Let us keep up with that high standard.

As men, books also look for a home. *Your* home should be *their* home.

Comments at Cilician Catholicate's Fourth Annual Book Fair, 1981.

Visiting President Ronald Reagan in Washington, D.C., 1983.

*T*he spirit blows at all times and in all places. Those who have their ears open and clean may hear its voice. No one can know where it comes from and where it leads. Those who have their minds transparent, their hearts pure and their wills set aright may follow, for they believe that it leads to where God wants us to be and what God wants us to do.
Not Fiction, 1990

I end with the wisdom of a great, great philosopher, theologian and church father. Centuries ago, this great thinker and profound theologian, St. Augustine, said, "Without us, God will not. Without God, we, human beings, cannot. And without us, God will not." Very humbly, I would like to add, "without us working together, hand in hand, neither God nor we will benefit."
The Challenge of Secularism in the Middle East, 1994

President George Bush welcomes His Holiness Vazken I and His Holiness Karekin II to the White House, February 1989.

We live in the present times as the descendants of our ancestors whose legacy, the Church of Armenia, continues to play a leading role in our entire national life both in Armenia, our motherland, and in the Diaspora. We have not inherited the Church for the sake of preserving it as a precious possession. We are under the sacred obligation of continuing our life within and through the process of the Church's ongoing and never-ending mission. We are not the masters, but the stewards and the servants. Often, we are tempted to speak so much of the past that we become the victims of thinking of the Church as a glorious heritage to be treasured and cherished. There is a great deal of truth and validity in this approach. For in a sense the church is a living memory. But the whole truth and the genuine authenticity go further beyond.

The Church: Our Life, 1981.

A rare complete family photograph: Back row, left to right, Zohrab Sarkissian, Sona Sarkissian, Vehapar's brother and sister-in-law; Yester Sarkissian, Vehapar's sister. Front row, left to right, Taline Sarkissian, niece; Ovsanna Sarkissian, mother; His Holiness; Hagop Sarkissian, father; and nephew Hagop Sarkissian.

There is an appealing word in the golden chain of the Beatitudes as registered by St. Matthew (5:9): "Blessed are the peacemakers, for they will be called sons of God." Our Heavenly Teacher considers blessed not so much the *peacelovers*, desirous of peace, but rather the *peacemakers*: those who dispel the disorder, disentangle complex crises through such positive actions that prevent antagonism and seditious behavior. Therefore, according to the message of the "Prince of Peace," men and women are called to put all their energies into action for the creation and preservation of peace.

And this not only in times of war, but also in times of normal conditions and situations where, apart from war, so many other factors make havoc because they give way to moral abuses, exploitations and injustices that disturb our life both in its outward setting and in its inner dimensions. Often in our so-called normal conditions of life, under the surface of what looks peaceful, ordinary, orderly, people experience inner troubles and encounter inner disturbances which sometimes are harder to bear than calamities imposed from the outside world or caused by external factors.

Blessed are the Peacemakers, 1991.

At the end of the day Vehapar retreats to his office to read and write.

155

*L*et us water the tree of faith. The tree of faith is the Church and the water is our sweat, the sweat of honest labor shed for rebuilding and revitalizing our Church. ... Without light the world is merely a blind existence; in like manner, without spiritual and intellectual light, our souls become blind entities.
Shoghakn, 1997.

THE JOURNEY BEGINS

*I*n the beginning of my studies at the seminary, I suffered from being far from my family; but little by little, it became that home to me.... At that age, I could not really think, in a responsible way, about the vocation, but I entered. Then, obviously, I thought a lot about the vocation, but that reflection developed in the spiritual and intellectual environment of the seminary....

I must admit that above all it [entering the seminary] was the desire to study. In my village, there were not so many possibilities for my future; we did not have a secondary school. So I had begun my apprenticeship with the tailor, since I wanted to help my father with the very modest economic conditions in which we were living. But it was then that Father Movses offered me the possibility of going to the seminary. He told me that after my studies, they would ask me if I wanted to become a priest or not; in fact my desire to become a priest was not something that anyone could have predicted. The idea of the vocation developed slowly inside of me, during my six years in the seminary, where, first, I completed my secondary studies, then theology, philosophy, and Armenology. As the idea developed, prayer and my participation in liturgical life had a very important influence on me, as well as a more profound look at the Christian tradition, of biblical and patristic literature. The spiritual values, which, in the beginning, I was unable to grasp through reason, penetrated my being, were internalized, assumed.

...There were times when I felt alone. I would ask myself, "Why is it that such or such a project, fundamentally beneficial to our church and our people, has not become reality? Where is God?" This moment of doubt, of hesitation, is a part of my experience. But I have never truly struggled with God in the sense of a rebellion. God is incontestable, and it is our duty not

With his namesake, Karekin I Hovsepiantz, Catholicos of the Great House of Cilicia. The future Karekin II of Cilicia and Karekin I of Etchmiadzin is on the right.

Bishop Karekin visits Rev. Fr. Movses and Yetetzgin Shrikian. Rev. Fr. Movses is the priest who suggested that the young Nishan Sarkissian leave Kessab and go to Beirut to study at the Seminary in Antelias. In later years His Holiness wrote about this occasion in his book Khorhe yev Medir (Think and Enter), part of which is printed in the beginning of this book.

to stray from Him because solitude is like hell on earth.... There were times when I did not want to accept certain events, and I could not believe that they were part of God's will. That was the case when Catholicos Zareh I of Cilicia died, the victim of a heart attack, at the age of forty-eight. He was such a saintly and devoted man that his death sickened me. I asked myself why such a person could so suddenly vanish forever. I was affected by it, became ill. But, in the end, I said, "God is greater." Similar moments of Gethsemane are part of our human existence; Jesus survived the moment when he prayed, "Father, let this cup be far from me." All the same, he added, "Let your will be done."
Between Heaven and Earth, 1999

In 1930 the Catholicosate of Cilicia was established in Antelias, Lebanon. As new possibilities were now being created for the Catholicosate of Cilicia, the Catholicos Sahak I Khabayan, already advanced in age and being deeply affected by the great sufferings of his people during the First World War, called Archbishop Babgen Guleserian—again one of the first graduates of Armash Seminary—to assist him in his efforts to rebuild a new ecclesiastical and national life in the new countries of the Diaspora.... His five years as catholicos marked a time of intensive work which resulted in concrete achievements such as the establishment of a seminary directed by another graduate of the seminary of Armash, Vardapet Shahe Gasparian, the founding of a printing press, and the publication of a monthly review under the name of *Hask* (Ear of Corn) which was accompanied by the publication of religious, educational and historical brochures and books. After his premature death in 1936 the archbishop of Cyprus, Petros Sarajian, was appointed vicar-

*With fellow seminarians and their teachers.
Very Rev. Fr. Karekin is on extreme right.*

*In his dormitory room in Antelias with his classmate
who later became Archbishop Ardavast Terterian.*

general and later, in 1940, succeeded the aged catholicos Sahak, when the latter passed away in 1939. His short reign as vicar general and as catholicos proved greatly beneficial in the sphere of building. The cathedral at Antelias, the memorial chapel of the Armenian Martyrs, and the seminary building together with the residence of the catholicos were built through his wise administration and tireless efforts.

The Second World War halted this constructive activity. But after 1945, when Catholicos Karekin I Hovsepiantz came to the throne, a new period of spiritual and intellectual awakening dawned upon the Armenian Church. During his reign of seven years, the Catholicosate of Cilicia flourished primarily in cultural activities. The catholicos himself being a great scholar encouraged the higher studies in the seminary and gave impetus to the publishing work. The monthly review, *Hask*, was enriched in content and was enlarged in scope. The number of theological students was increased. New items were added to the curriculum together with the addition of two years to the course of study. Well-qualified professors were invited to join the faculty. The scope of the catholicosate's work was extended as new priests were sent to various parts of the world to serve the parishes and dioceses.

....

Four years elapsed between his death and the election of his successor, Catholicos Zareh I (1956). The first graduate of the seminary of Antelias, he was an experienced church leader in Syria having served as primate of Aleppo for sixteen years. During his short-lived reign many beneficial achievements were accomplished. The catholicosate's

*At the blessing of the Holy Chrism (Muron) with fellow students.
Very Rev. Fr. Karekin is second from left.*

*Very Rev. Fr. Karekin (seated, left) with Archbishop Terenig Poladian (seated, center)
Dean of the Seminary, and seminarians.*

work was extended to those Armenian communities in the Diaspora that had been in desperate need of spiritual care for many years.... The seminary was given much encouragement. His personal insight and saintly life had a determining influence on all the students who readily entered the service of the church by joining the religious community of the catholicosate. The relations of the Cilician see with other churches and governments of the Middle East were strengthened through his leadership. He can be rightly described as the ecumenical figure *par excellence* of the Armenian Church in the Middle East.

The Armenian Church in Contemporary Times, 1969

When I was teaching at the seminary, I considered my colleagues and students to be my family; it was the same thing with the people I served as a priest or as a bishop. Besides, I have always had friends on whom I can depend, people whom I could always ask for advice if I had a problem. As for the rest, I have tried to keep a sort of solitude; it is something that has become second nature

Keeping vigil at the funeral of Catholicos Karekin I Hovsepiantz, 1952.

Very Rev. Fr. Karekin (standing) with, (seated left to right), Archbishop Khoren, Catholicos Zareh I, and Archbishop Ghevont.

to me. Often my friends tell me that in spite of my commitment to others, I am still lonely. I would say that I am alone, but not lonely or isolated. Here is my recipe for monastic life: full social engagement, but in keeping room for yourself; and also, having friends with whom you can share your joys as well as your troubles.
Between Heaven and Earth, 1999

What is unique to the Armenian Church is its national spirit, its strong national character and mission. Without these characteristics, it is impossible to imagine the Armenian Church in the service of God's kingdom and the history of mankind and it is futile to expect of it any lasting results.
Hask, 1969.

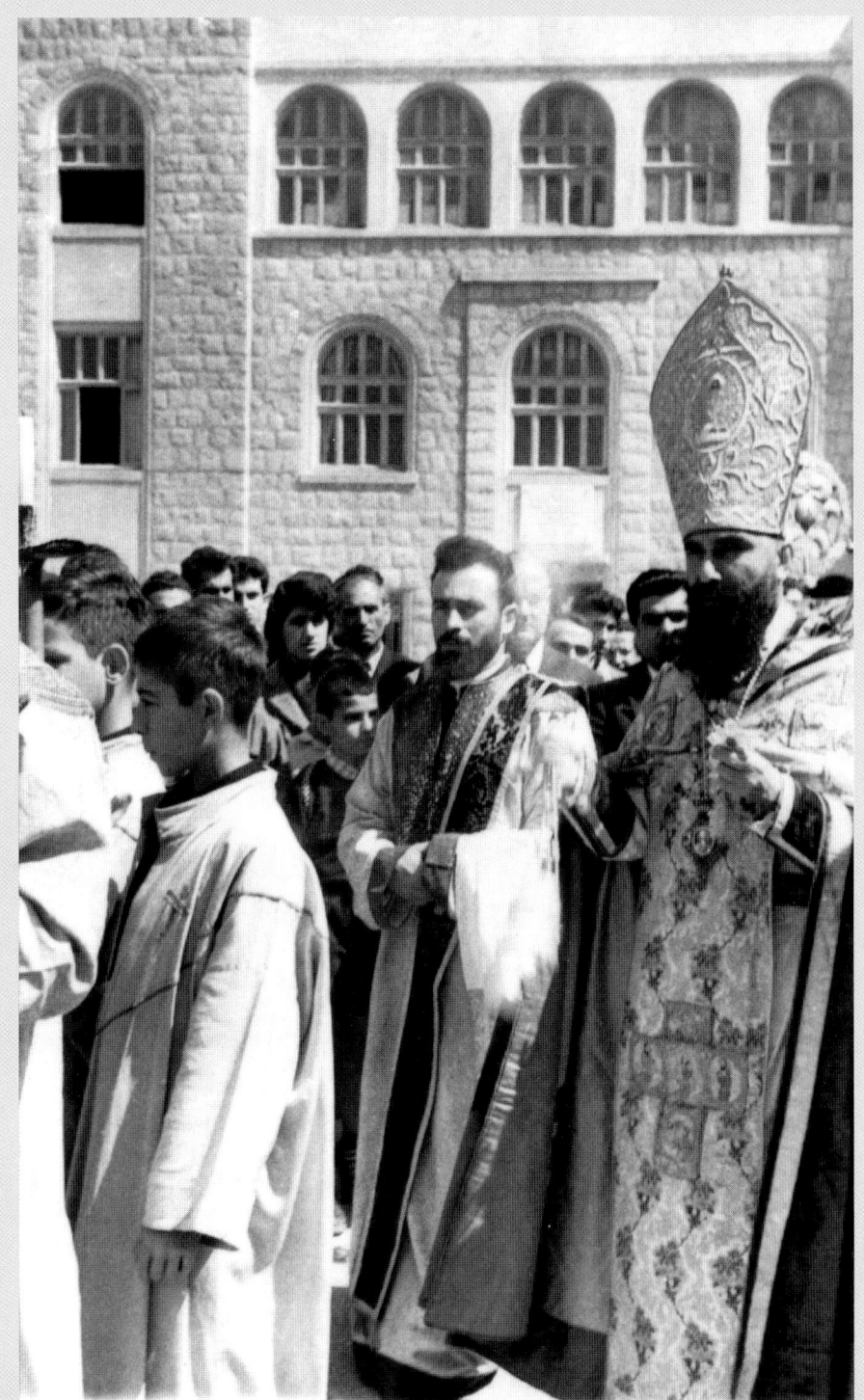
With Catholicos Zareh I. Very Rev. Fr. Karekin is on the left next to the Catholicos.

I arrived in Oxford in October 1957. The main purpose of my coming to England was...to further my studies in Dogmatic Theology and Church History. As I was already teaching the same subjects in the Armenian Theological Seminary in Antelias, Lebanon, I thought my visit to this country would help me to acquire a wider knowledge of these subjects for my later work in the same Seminary.

I think I was very fortunate to be placed in Wycliffe Hall, Oxford. This is a Church of England Theological College for the training of Anglican clergy. The students here have easy access to the University lectures, which later proved to be extremely helpful to me in connection with my lecturing work in the Seminary.

The first term of my first year I devoted to the study of the history of the Church of England under the guidance of the Chaplain of Wycliffe Hall. This was very useful first in understanding my environment in its historical background. And, I must say, history or tradition is present in England as much as the daily life itself. You can see it, you can feel it in every corner in Oxford and in almost any place on this island! The sense of history is perhaps part of the English character; I had to understand it.

At the end of the second term I was accepted by the Board of the Theological Faculty as a post-graduate student, a candidate for the degree of B.Litt. The subject of the thesis for this degree had to have an ecumenical significance. I chose the following theme: "The Council of Chalcedon and the Armenian Church." In fact, as it is well known, the Council of Chalcedon is the chief—if not the only—cause of the separation between the Greek Orthodox and Armenian churches. The latter rejects the Council of Chalcedon which is accepted by the former as the "Fourth Ecumenical Council." So I decided to study the

A photograph of his class in Oxford University. Very Rev. Fr. Karekin is in the second row from bottom, fourth person from left.

historical and theological reasons for the rejection of the Council of Chalcedon by the Armenian Church and to try to see a possible way of reconciliation between these churches.

This being the basic idea in my mind I applied to the Theological Committee of the British Council of Churches asking them to make an extension of my scholarship for a second year since I had to stay in Oxford for six residential terms according to the regulations of the University. I was very grateful to them for their approval of my application.

Since then the center of my academic work became my thesis. I had to do much research work in the historical and theological documents of the fifth century both in relation to the Council of Chalcedon and to Armenian history and literature. I have now completed that part of the work and already written the first three chapters of the thesis, which have been approved by my supervisor. I hope to finish it during this summer, when I am staying in Oxford most of the time, and submit it to the Board in the Michaelmas term which is the sixth term and will be the last of my residence in Oxford.

If everything goes well, I hope, with God's will and help, I may get the degree in December and immediately return to Lebanon, where I will be resuming my previous work of teaching with further responsibilities.

…

The College was my home in the real sense of the word. After the first two months it had already become a familiar place to live in with friends. I tried to take part in almost all the important aspects of college life. I learned many things through this integration of my life into

Episcopal consecration by Khoren I, 1964.

the atmosphere of the college. The friendship, fellowship, private discussions—all these taught me things that I would never be able to get from anywhere else.

...

On the spiritual ground I was again fortunate in being in an Anglican College of Evangelical tradition. The whole atmosphere of worship here was entirely different from my own church's liturgical tradition. I was in a "foreign land!" But I liked to be in a "foreign land" in order to see it more closely and to understand it more deeply. Gradually it became more familiar to me. I began to enjoy parts of it and to sympathize with it. However different it is from my own church tradition and personal experience I feel now that I understand it.... And although still I feel much more at home in my own church with its deeply touching liturgical ethos, yet I can pray with an "evangelical" Christian with a complete sense of fellowship and spiritual partnership.

...

However, Oxford was not an "ivory tower" in which I could find the enjoyment of knowledge in a complete isolation from the world.
I came out from this "ivory tower" from time to time, mostly during the vacations, and I went to various places in England and saw the church's work on the spot.

First...I wanted to see something of the monastic life in the Church of England. In fact, I visited four of the main religious communities of the Church of England, which in their

Simon Vratzian, the last Prime Minister of the first Armenian Republic, congratulates the newly consecrated Bishops Ardavast and Karekin.

own ways opened to me new aspects of Christian spirituality. I was also able to go and see some theological colleges other than my own here in Oxford.

...I visited some parishes and some non-conformist churches in this country. It was a great opportunity for me to learn things about the pastoral task of the church as carried on in different ways by various particular churches and denominations. To see the people, to talk with them, to understand their own problems, to realize their own approach to the task of the church in this world—all these contributed very largely to my understanding of the vocation of the church in today's human situation.

I was given also the opportunity of speaking to people about my own church and about the problems of Christianity in the Middle East. It was a thrilling experience for me to stand on an Anglican or Congregational pulpit and to preach the word of God in a foreign language to a foreign congregation with whom my relation was only through the fellowship of the Christian faith, which we shared together.

...I would say that after my experience and studies in this country I have begun to understand my own Church, but this time in a different setting from that in which I had seen and known until now. That new setting is the vision of the Church Universal. If we begin to see the vision, then, I am sure, we are on the way to its actual realization. The unity of the church cannot come, humanly speaking, until and unless this vision is seen and felt by all Christians.

Excerpts from a personal report to the Scholarship Committee of the World Council of Churches, 1959.

A portrait with his proud parents following his Episcopal Consecration.1964.

I was the bishop of the south of the country [Iran], since New Julfa, which is close to Isfahan, is actually the headquarters of the Armenian bishop of the South of Iran. In the seventeenth century, Isfahan was the capital of the Safavid dynasty, built by Shah Abbas, who had convinced more than a thousand Armenians to leave their native land and to move to Persia to work on the construction of his palaces and magnificent architectural works, and to participate in its commerce. That's why New Julfa was, at that time, the spiritual center of the Armenian people of Iran as well as the episcopal center of the Far East. Armenians living in India, Indonesia, Singapore and other eastern countries were all part of that diocese.

When Teheran became the capital, the archbishopric moved there; New Julfa remained a cultural center, possessing a remarkable collection of seven hundred manuscripts, a museum, etc. So, outside of my pastoral ministry serving the Armenians of the southern regions of Iran, I was very concerned with our precious cultural heritage.

Opening of the renovated library of All Saviors Monastery, New Julfa, 1972.

. . . $\mathcal{A}$merican life was not foreign to me; the Anglo-Saxon tradition that I had become acquainted with in England had given me an idea of how life would be in America. Besides, during the years that I was active in the ecumenical movement at the World Council of Churches, I had met many American theologians, and when I was a bishop in Iran, I had traveled to America to develop our relations.

So in 1973, when I was named bishop in New York, I wasn't completely ignorant of American life; I can even say that I had a certain familiarity with it. So that change from Iran to America was not as traumatizing as one might think. As an Armenian bishop, I have, for the most part, shared the lives of the followers of the Armenian Church in the United States; but I have also kept abreast of the American ecclesiastical milieu, like the National Council of Churches of the United States, as well as other ecumenical, Catholic, Orthodox and Protestant circles.

Between Heaven and Earth, 1999

$\mathcal{W}$e are a *living* nation. Having journeyed through the valley of the shadow of death, having passed the test of genocide, we are now called to pass the test of a meaningful, fruitful, creative, productive life, in service to the same cause for which the martyrs dedicated their existence at the cost of their lives.

Two days ago, when I was visiting the Kellogg Center in Lansing, Michigan, I was deeply challenged by the beautiful golden inscription taken from the words of Abraham Lincoln. It read: "It is for us, the living…to be dedicated here to the unfinished task."

Ecumenical visitors are given a tour of All Saviors Monastery in New Julfa, 1972.

Always with books.

Yes—we have an unfinished task. A sacred legacy has been transmitted to us through the sacrifice of the martyrs, sealed by their own blood, as the supreme manifestation of their love for and dedication to the highest ideals of our Christian faith, national identity and dignity. This is not an easy task—particularly at this time, when such ideals are no longer held in the same high regard as in the days of the martyrs we venerate today—because they were men and women who through their lives on earth gave tangible expression of their faithfulness at the price of their sacrificial blood.

Such a life of dedication is a costly affair. It requires a sacrificial spirit, a courageous stand, living heroism. Here is where the Cross finds its proper meaning in our nation life....

More difficult has become that task as we continue our life in our predicament of a diaspora, where we constantly confront the temptation and the threat of assimilation. How do we maintain our identity in the midst of a world where we live under cultural and social conditions of the most varied and complex kinds?

For the last sixty years we have faced this challenge. Yet our ideal has not been eclipsed. On the contrary, there is a new and growing awareness of our identity and dignity as a distinct nation....

This is a time to give thanks to God for having granted us a new beginning with this new era of renaissance. Let us be worthy sons and daughters of that nation of Mount Ararat; let us be worthy of those who, for long centuries and under the hardest conditions of life, did not lose their identity, their faith and their national dignity.

Is it not a genuine source of joy to realize that for more than two thousand years we *did* overcome all tribulations, persecutions, devastations and massacres? Therefore, we should never give up hope. No one can predict the future course of human history. We live in hope, which is sustained by dedication. And let us never forget that both hope and dedication are rooted in faith.

Living Martyrdom, 1975

ECUMENICAL JOURNEY

I vividly remember the pale pages of a modest publication—a bunch of typed sheets attached together, really—which was the first non-Armenian journal I ever subscribed to as a young deacon and priest. It came from France, I think: a news bulletin from the center of *Istina* (the French ecumenical quarterly), edited by Fr. Dumont. In those simple pages, I learned so much about the ecumenical movement! I was just fascinated by what I discovered there, and regarded it as a breath of fresh air in theological literature and in Christian life generally. It was predominantly oriented toward spiritual and theological trends....

We young students and priests were trying to look further, to search deeper, in a quest for our own understanding of the unity and mission of the Church. We were also trying to march towards the recovery of that unity: a goal that still seems so essential to the credibility of the Christian faith in the world at large. How fortunate I feel now—and how grateful I am to God—that He kindled in us, at that early stage in our ministries, the spirit of this new era, with its renewed sense of openness and committed fellowship.

Throughout the past forty-six years, my priestly life has coincided with my ecumenical engagement. I was a sixteen-year-old deacon when the ecumenical movement reached its decisive moment in 1948, with the creation of the World Council of Churches in Amsterdam. This was succeeded by another great event, the Lund Conference on Faith and Order, which I followed very closely in the press and literature. But my real baptism in the ecumenical movement took place in Beirut, Lebanon, in 1955. There, at the Conference of Christian Youth Leaders in the Middle East, I was able to see for the first time such great figures as Dr. Willem Visser 't Hooft, Dr. Philip Potter and others.

Speaking at World Conference on Church and Society, July 1966, sponsored by the World Council of Churches, Geneva, with the participation of theologians and laymen. It was the first ecumenical conference to convene dealing exclusively with social questions since 1937. The Very Rev. Fr. Karekin Sarkissian is addressing the gathering. At this time he was the Dean of the Cilician Seminary.

The conference was organized under the auspices of the World Council of Churches' Youth Department, and it attracted many young Christian leaders. Patriarch Ignatius IV Hazim, the late Bishop Samuel of the Coptic Church, Metropolitan George Khodre and other young priests, as well as laymen such as Albert Laham, were all actively participating. It was my first experience sharing prayers, ideas, meals and simple conversation with people who neither spoke my language, nor were familiar with my own church's life and liturgical experience. Yet I felt at home with them. A certain inner disposition, a kind of sympathetic inclination, is conducive to better understanding and true communion in the ecumenical movement—and for that matter in any human encounter or relationship. In retrospect, I think that my experiences at that meeting have had a crucial significance and impact over my whole life. I would even go so far as to say that it proved to be a decisive meeting, a kind of turning point: every participant felt that something was happening in his own person. A new breeze was blowing over that younger generation of church servants. Years later, when I read Dr. Visser t'Hooft's account of the conference in his memoirs, I was struck (as always) by the discerning mind of that prophetic figure, but also by the great faith he had possessed in that young generation of the Eastern and Oriental Orthodox churches. This is what he observed, with his usual perspicacity, at our 1955 gathering: "This visit to the Near East ended at a conference in Beirut, at which representatives of the younger generation of their member churches in the Near East met under the auspices of the World Council's Youth Department. Here something new was being born. Here, there was a common concern for the Christian witness and Christian action. The day of renewal of life was being prepared in the oldest churches of Christendom.

More than four hundred delegates from eighty nations participated in the World Conference on Church and Society. Geneva, 1966.

As for myself, this first, impact-making meeting aroused in me the profound conviction that the cause of Christian unity was inseparably linked with the renewal of the Church. In the years that followed, I pursued opportunities for higher theological education at Oxford, while participating in ecumenical gatherings of greater scope and responsibility. And my conviction only deepened.

Later in life, by the grace of God, the World Council of Churches would offer me even greater opportunities for ecumenical activity: serving on its Faith and Order Commission; attending four General Assemblies…sitting on the World Council's Central and Executive Committees for fourteen years—seven as vice-moderator; participating in the Second Vatican Council and the 1968 Lambeth Conference; organizing, together with my brethren such as Abba Paulos Gregorios, the 1965 Addis Ababa Conference of the Heads of the Oriental Orthodox Churches; visiting many churches—Orthodox, Catholic and Protestant—in many parts of the world; delivering lectures, writing articles, and conversing with responsible people in the Christian Church, as well as with leaders from other religions, the academy and the political realm. It has been a great variety of experiences; and through them all, I have come to see that the content of the ecumenical movement is multi-faceted. The quest for unity never ceases to occupy the central place, but it does not exist in isolation.

The quest for unity drove me (as it has so many others) closer to the source of our faith: Jesus Christ, His Gospel and the constitutive tradition of His Church. As you draw closer to that source, the vision of Christian unity strikes you with great clarity….

…

Speaking with Pope John XXIII during the Second Vatican Council, 1962.

Of course, ecumenical openness is not meant to nullify our critical abilities. The encounter itself is only the beginning of a greater process of discernment and distinction; it is a means to choice and rejection. We are told that in the fields of the Lord, the "wheat" and the "weed" grow together. The enemy is keen to sow the weed; our task is to separate it from the wheat. The ecumenical movement has a role in that task as well (indeed, the disagreements, dissensions and conflicts within the World Council of Churches are an indication of that role). The temptation is great to reduce the ecumenical encounter to mere sentimentality, on the one hand, or zealotry on the other. Both approaches are shallow, it seems to me, because they concentrate on the temporal aspect of our mutual relations, and disregard that critical function which is the only way to make a real impact on, and reap enduring benefits for, the participating churches. The integrity of the ecumenical movement resides in this challenging function. Indeed, an easy ecumenism may be no ecumenism at all.

...

Throughout my years of participation within the fold of the World Council, we have endlessly bemoaned the fact that there is still a gap between, on the one hand, what happens in the meetings and activities of the WCC, and on the other, what happens in the daily, grass-roots lives of our member churches. Indeed, the people in the pews are not adequately cognizant of the true dimensions and significance of the ecumenical movement. From the perspective of an ordinary church, the ecumenical arena is like an alien world. So-called "ecumenical affairs" are the special province of an elite:

Visiting Markarios III, Greek Orthodox Prelate and President of Cyprus.

the "ecumenists." They perform their work "out there"—in various parts of the world which have almost no relation to anything happening "in here," in the actual life of a church, in the inner mansions of the House of God. Given this situation, misunderstandings are practically inevitable.

It is high time we took this challenge seriously. And by "we" I mean the member churches themselves, who need to initiate this ecumenical pastoralia, with whatever assistance is necessary from the World Council. After all, the target of all our efforts is the people of God, for whose sake our Lord assumed human nature and put on "the form of a servant."

...

The fiftieth anniversary of the World Council of Churches should inspire the Christian churches to a deeper commitment, both to our internal ecumenical sphere, as well as to our action in the outer world. Periodic reassessments and re-orientations are part of the existential ethos of the World Council, and are indispensable to its sound operation. "Aggiornamento" has always been an item on its agenda. As long as we are fortified by an unshakable spirit of fellowship, I am confident that we can overcome the internal stresses of the present day. Let us renew the covenant we accepted half a century ago, for the sake of the unity of the Church, and in the spirit of the mission entrusted to us by Christ.

I am reminded that the emblem of the World Council of Churches is a boat with the cross at its center, floating above the waves. More often than not, this world has provided us with turbulent waters on which to navigate. But we struggle on, even though our harbor is not on this earth. The ecumenical movement,

Arriving at the Vatican for meetings, October 1965.

indeed unity itself, is a means, but hardly a *raison d'etre*. After all, a united Church is only a vessel, through which the world may believe that Jesus Christ is "the Way, the Truth and the Life."
...And the Boat Moves on the Waters, 1998

What do we understand when we use the word "ecumenical"? It is no longer a strange word to be looked up in the dictionary. Once primarily a denizen of ecclesiastical circles, today the word "ecumenical" has acquired citizenship in the lexicon of the secular press.

As used in the Byzantine empire, "ecumenical" meant universal, in the sense of "the inhabited world." The Greek word *oikoumene* means the inhabited world, the civilized world, as contrasted with the barbarian world, which is not part of the *oikoumene*. It is in this sense that we refer to the formal gatherings of the early Christian Church as the "Ecumenical Councils."

The term and its variants were adopted in the twentieth century to designate a movement whose goal was to recover the sense of the totality of the Christian family, to restore the bond of unity that Christ gave us through His incarnation and ministry. Even so, "ecumenism" does not primarily refer to the formal discussions among theologians regarding Christian unity. "Ecumenism," as I understand it, refers to a spirit, a way of looking at Christian life, where we recognize that all Christians are bound in brotherhood through the unique figure of Christ and the unique nature of His Gospel. It is a common effort to grow in our understanding of the Truth, to act under the imperative of love, and to share our gifts in the service of those whose lives are improved through such sharing. Ultimately, this becomes a self-enriching way of praising God and partaking in His kingdom.

....

Above: Welcoming dignitaries from Iran. At right is the Prime Minister of Iran, His Excellency Abbas Hoveida, 1962.

Right: Greeting His Majesty Haile Selassie I, Emperor of Ethiopia, with Rev. Dr. Eugene Carson Blake, General Secretary of the World Council of Churches, 1965.

When speaking about ecumenism or the ecumenical movement, many people instinctively associate the whole movement with the World Council of Churches, or with some other organization. Well, let me affirm from the outset that the ecumenical movement is neither bound nor consumed by any institutional apparatus. It is manifested through a variety of efforts undertaken in common by Christians throughout the world. To be sure, the World Council is a distinct and (in my experience) the most significant effort among others; but the ecumenical movement should not be equated or totally identified with the World Council of Churches.

Nor did ecumenism even begin with the World Council. The trend towards ecumenism has been a part and parcel of the Church from its very beginning. In the deeply spiritual, extremely moving and tremendously challenging seventeenth chapter of the Gospel of St. John, we see its true source in one of Christ's most moving prayers. In that passage, Jesus prays that His followers (in the first place the apostles themselves) may all be one....

...

As one of our patriarchs, Catholicos Zareh I of Antelias, now of blessed memory, once put it: "Today it is not the form of the faith that is in question. Today the faith itself is at stake." That is all I am trying to say. If our Christian faith means anything to us, it must be shared with all people; until that happens (maybe in order for it to happen) it must be manifested for all people. The universality of the Christian faith is an intrinsic part of its nature. The ecumenical movement is our endeavor to bring that universality to life through the unity of our Church.

The World Council of Churches in its New Dimension and the Orthodox Churches
lecture delivered 1978

Above: With the distinguished ecumenist Dr. Willem Visser't Hooft, a Founder and General Secretary of the World Council of Churches, early 1960s.

Right: The Rev. Edward Scott, head of the Anglican Church of Canada, and Moderator of the World Council of Churches, welcomes His Holiness to Geneva, 1977, shortly after his election and consecration to the Cilician throne.

*I*n 1961, His Grace Bishop Willebrands, not yet a cardinal, came to Antelias to speak with the Catholicos at that time, the great Catholicos Zareh I, who was endowed with an exemplary ecumenical spirit. Very delicately, he asked him the following question, more or less in these terms: In case the Pope convenes a Council in the Vatican and invites a representative from our church, would we be ready to participate? And our Catholicos replied immediately: "But does a man who invites his brother doubt that he will accept?" That was the feeling of unity that he had. Then he added: "If we synthesize all of the teachings of the Gospel in one hundred points, don't you think that we would agree on ninety-nine of them? However, unfortunately, we often only talk about the one point on which our opinions separate us, forgetting how much we have in common...." He pointed to the wall before him: "If there were a little black spot on this white wall, we would forget the whiteness of the wall to talk about the little stain...."

What I learned is that today, we must, ... look at what unites us. For me, this is the true strategy—if I can speak so—of ecumenism, which must allow us to move into the third millennium.

Between Heaven and Earth, 1999

With Pope Paul VI at the Vatican, 1965.

*I*n the course of our two months' stay and contacts in the Vatican, we realized that our presence was taken much more seriously than we ever expected before going to Rome. It is true that we were not even well prepared for the task in which we actually found ourselves involved. In other words, our presence there was considered not as something conventional or merely marginal, but something really important being accompanied with expectations for effective influence. Therefore, the reception we found in the Vatican exceeded the limits of pure conventional courtesy and friendly atmosphere. It was converted into a sort of dialogue, that is to say, an opening to each other in a real concern for each other. We never fell into the temptation of entering in the slightest way into a conversation as negotiators, as representatives for such an official task. We always felt ourselves as witnesses to our own faith and traditions. And it is right to say, I believe, that we were approached by our hosts and by the bishops of the Council in that same position. We gradually became, so to speak, a factor in their deliberations simply by our presence and witness. We were treated by the Roman Church officials and the conciliar bishops in such a way that we never felt anything being offensive to our own tradition. On the contrary, even in cases where the bishops knew that our views and attitudes were different they formulated their own views in such a way that any criticism or offense could be avoided.

It was with a real sense of grief that I realized how the Eastern Churches were still unknown in the largest circles of the Episcopal body of the Roman Catholic Church. Except some parts of the Continent, and some groups among the European bishops, the large groups of Italian, Spanish, South American, African and North American bishops were almost completely ignorant about our Eastern Churches. To many of them the presence

With Dr. Phillip Potter, Secretary General of the World Council of Churches, in Geneva, 1977. At this time His Holiness was Vice Moderator of the WCC.

of observers from the Eastern Churches opened a whole new world of Christian tradition that they had never known before. The contact opened their eyes which could see beyond the dead letter of the books. Of course, nothing was achieved in terms of concrete, substantial results. This was a start. But I am sure that they first realized that Roman Catholicism was not everything in Christianity that Eastern Christian tradition was to be taken seriously and, second, they received a stimulus to know better the Eastern Churches through readings and contacts. Indeed, our presence there served as a living introduction to further study of and relationship with Eastern Christendom.

It would be wrong to press this last remark to such a point that one may think that there was a complete ignorance about Eastern Churches. The "Sacred Congregation on Eastern Churches" within the Roman Curia itself and the many studies carried on by individual historians, theologians, liturgists, as well as by special centers and reviews have opened the Christian world to the Roman Catholic mind and knowledge.

...

There is a margin of the Council that cannot be left as blank paper! A note is called for. The consultations and talks with the bishops and many theologians, historians, canonists, liturgists—a whole group of experts—outside the Council proved most valuable and in many ways useful. They opened contacts that will continue in the future. It is above all doubt that these people have the real and greatest influence on the Roman Catholic Church's doctrinal positions and ecumenical attitudes.

....

Above: His Holiness and Austrian Prelate, Cardinal Franciscus Koenig, with Elias Sarkis, President of Lebanon, 1978.

Right: With Dr. Geoffrey Fisher, Archbishop of Canterbury.

... I feel after two months spent in Rome in close touch and association with the Second Vatican Council, the presence of Eastern observers is an act of faithfulness to their own tradition. It is a sacred duty to proclaim what we believe to be the truth. The Second Vatican Council is an invitation for such a proclamation to be done not in terms of pride and "missionary" attitudes, but in terms of service and for the purpose of mutual understanding in our common witness to Christ's will for the unity of His Church and His message and command for the evangelization of the world.
Personal Notes of an Observer-Delegate to the II Vatican Council, 1963.

I can never forget one moving moment that I experienced while attending the Second Vatican Council some four years ago. It was the moment when the Ethiopian Catholic Church was celebrating the Ethiopian liturgy in the Basilica of St. Peter, in Rome. The Pope himself was attending the Liturgy. We observers, who were given a place near the altar, suddenly realized that almost all the Catholic bishops of Africa, most of them indigenous people from various countries of the African continent, had left their seats and approached the altar with intense curiosity and in hopeful expectation! They were eager and anxious to see how a liturgy, the highest moment in a Christian's life, the supreme Christian act, could be performed in a purely African setting, with African language and singing, vestments of national shape, musical instruments of local use, and actions all pertaining to the African manners and indigenous ways of life. The Schema of the liturgy was being discussed in that session of the Council. The African Catholic bishops were

His Holiness with Archbishop Tiran Nersoyan. The two Church leaders, both eminent scholars, developed a close friendly relationship, 1983.

earnestly and vigorously arguing for greater freedom to introduce and incorporate national cultural elements in the liturgical life of their church. The Ethiopian liturgy provided them the best and richest illustration in support of their views and a guarantee for the fulfillment of their aspirations!
The Witness of the Oriental Orthodox Churches, 1968

One day when I was in Geneva, in the World Council of Churches headquarters, and I was asked to be the preacher for that morning's service of the executive committee, I chose this theme of dedication. I didn't know then what the response would be. But from representatives of all the churches from around the world—from Russia to Asia, from Africa to Europe and North America, South America, there were people present and they responded in this way: Dedication, that is the response to our human crisis today. Because there is the crisis of agony of the world, there is the crisis of emptiness among the youth in Europe. What is the meaning of life? What do we live for? We have everything, we have food, we have clothes, we have shelter, we have pleasure, we have everything. Then what? What is the meaning? What is the quality of life? That is the big question today among the youth, particularly in Europe. And the emptiness of life is hell on earth, which is giving rise to so many meaningless movements in the whole world. I believe today that the meaning of life is that self-dedication, the self-disclosure, the self-realization for the sake of others.
Challenge to Continue, a dialogue with the youth,
Princeton Club, 1983

His Holiness with the Archbishop of Canterbury, Dr. Robert Runcie.

They are not saints who refrain from entering in life for fear of encountering evil.... They are not saints who remain in their individual isolation, motionless and idle, and reduce their lives, with the emptiness of their souls, to a desert where marches do not exist because there is no water at all.

What saintliness is there in those hands that never touch life? While on the contrary, what a sacred charm emanates from those hands that though are dipped sometimes in the mire of life but do not get soiled; they come out purified and more beautiful.
In Witness of Blood, 1995.

Above: His Holiness Vazken I and His Holiness Karekin II with Rev. Dr. Jesse Jackson, in New York, 1989, following the December 1988 earthquake in northern Armenia.

Right: Greeting Cyrill III, Pope of Alexandria.

*D*eep in my heart, I sense that we are gradually departing from the early, authentic Christian standards for relating to the world. Our Lord Himself was accepted neither by the Jews of His time, nor by the Romans; He was rejected by the pious (whatever their religions) as well as the intellectuals of His day. The crucifixion was the world's response to His mission. And in later times, His apostles and their successors met no different reaction at the hands of the world. Yet they were courageous, bold, clear and firm in their Christian witness. It is true indeed, in the words of William Barclay, that "the man who is not willing to be different cannot be a Christian at all."

Face to Face with Ourselves, 1997.

Above: Karekin I with Alexy II, the Russian Patriarch. 1995.

Right: His Holiness with Pope Shenouda, Patriarch of the Coptic Church. 1995.

History tells us most eloquently how disastrous have been the consequences of the division of Eastern Churches because of the Council of Chalcedon and other related factors of a non-theological nature. Isolation has resulted in hard, staunch, exclusive, unyielding attitudes, which have led to the dislocation and the decompositon of the Eastern Christian world and have impaired its integrity and solidarity. Generally speaking in the past, polemics have dominated the relationship between the two groups of Churches. The self-defensive, self-justifying tendency and method, with the natural implication of mutual condemnation, have prevailed in the conversations that have taken place. Fresh attempts at a deeper understanding of each other's positions as expressed in the post-Chalcedonian theological tradition may greatly help us in our search for the recovery of the unity of the Eastern Churches.

That vision constitutes one of the major factors in this study, and that same vision must be, I believe, a driving force in all studies which may follow along the same lines.

Council of Chalcedon and the Armenian Church, 1965.

Karekin I with the Ecumenical Patriarch Bartholomew. At right is the Patriarch of Istanbul, His Beatitude Archbishop Mesrob Mutafian. 1996.

WCC Central Committee meeting, Geneva.

The Church is our essence, our bone and marrow. ... If you take the Church out of our history, tell me, what else will be left? Take away the fact that we have been the first nation to adopt Christianity; or the fact that it was the Church that created our alphabet; or that the first book ever written in the Armenian language was the Bible in the fifth century. Remove from our history the evidence that all our literature is inspired by the Christian experience and thinking; remove all the churches built throughout the centuries: Etchmiadzin, Varagavank, Geghardavank, Sanahin, Haghpat, Marmashen, Harijavank, Tatev, Hripsime, Gayane, and many others. Well, what will be left of our culture? Or take away our architecture, our Liturgy, our cross-stones, the manuscripts and miniature illuminations, and, tell me, what else shall we have to offer to the world? Our armies? Our victories? Our economic power? Where and when did we have them? ... Only moral values will make us great. We have not ruled by our economy, nor by the politics of our kingdoms. Whatever we have been, we have been by our spiritual values and our culture. Our Church has always been the only force that tutored and strengthened our soul and led us to victory.
Etchmiadzin, 1998.

1700th ANNIVERSARY

... Catholicos Vazken I, of blessed memory, and I talked at great length about how to celebrate the 1700th anniversary of the official proclamation of the Christian faith as the state national religion of our people in the year 301. Our discussions started in July 1988 when we were both in Moscow participating in the 1000th anniversary of the Russian Orthodox Church, which in itself, in terms of how it was celebrated, was highly significant of a changing world. Indeed, what happened at that time in Russia would have been unimaginable just a few years earlier. The Russian celebration acquired an ecumenical dimension with worldwide recognition and participation, which resulted in very positive changes for the Russian Church. Thousands of students enrolled in the seminaries; thousands of churches were reopened. The anniversary ushered in a period of revival and growth.

Vazken Vehapar and I hoped that our 1700th celebration would have a similar effect on our church. I tell you, I am looking forward to the year 2001 when the celebration will culminate in Armenia, when thousands of Armenians from all corners of the world will come to Armenia, when the new Cathedral in Yerevan which has already broken ground will be completed and consecrated and we will all together look to the bright future of our church and nation.

Taped Conversation, 1999

The end of the second millennium of the Christian era of history is drawing near. People and institutions, religious and secular, states, churches, international and ecumenical organizations are increasingly becoming engaged in a process of self-awareness of and self-inquiry in

Conference of Scholars, Paris, 1996. Always appreciative of scholars and scholarship, His Holiness invited internationally recognized scholars and specialists to attend a conference in Paris in order to receive their thoughts about the appropriate way to celebrate the 1700th anniversary of Christian Armenia.

their present day world predicament and of the future, however uncertain and unidentifiable it may look. Books are being written, symposia are being held, debates are taking place, statistics are being drawn-up, historical experiences are being analyzed, achievements are being assessed, failures are being identified and projections are being envisaged for future predictions.

The Armenian church and nation while sharing the concerns of their brethren and sisters around the world in this regard, have a particular reason and a unique opportunity to take the end of the second millennium and the dawning of the third very seriously and, indeed, in a distinctive manner. For, in fact, the first year of the third millennium will mark the 1700th anniversary of that greatest moment of Armenian history when the Christian faith was adopted by the king of Armenia, Tiridates III, and was proclaimed as the national religion of the Armenian people. It is a well known fact that in the very beginning of the 4th century Armenia through the baptism of its king and through the proclamation by the State recognized the Christian faith as its official, national religion.

The exact date of such formal acceptance has been a matter of debate among scholars, both Armenian and non-Armenian. Recent researches have acknowledged the years between 313 and 316 as the most probable date.

However, the question of date is of secondary importance for the purpose of the celebration of the 1700 years of Christian witness in Armenia and in the neighboring countries. The 2001 date is selected because the year 301 has always traditionally enjoyed the character of official acceptance. Indeed, the first year of the third millennium provides a most appropriate context for such celebration. In any case, as the *Oxford Dictionary of the Christian Church* puts it, "The Armenians were the first nation to adopt Christianity as their national religion."

…

The Cathedral of St. Gregory the Illuminator in Yerevan, built in honor of the milestone anniversary, seats 1,700 people and is the largest Armenian cathedral in the world. The idea of a grand cathedral in the capital city began with His Holiness Vazken I; His Holiness Karekin I presided over the groundbreaking and blessing and the beginning of construction; His Holiness Karekin II guided the completion of the Cathedral and officiated at the Consecration of the Cathedral during the impressive 1700th commemorative celebrations in September 2001.

The seventeen centuries of continuous, unbroken and creative witness of the Armenian Church is part of Christendom and of human history in general. The 17th centenary celebration is an excellent opportunity to bring that witness under international and pan-Christian focus. Particularly in this present age of world communication where the encounter of cultures has created a multi-cultural trend of dialogue and interchange, such a worldwide knowledge and recognition of Armenian Christian culture of spiritual, theological, liturgical, literary and artistic nature and content is not only possible but also important for an integral understanding of the relationship between Christian faith and human culture.

One of the most eloquent and characteristic words in modern philosophical, theological and sociological vocabulary is the word *inculturation*. How can the Armenian historical experience offer a valuable contribution to our present-day search for a true understanding of the interplay between religious faith and human culture? This is an area of investigation in which the Armenian Christian culture may cast some light.

I personally wanted from the very early stage when I, then as Catholicos of Cilicia, was discussing the 1700th anniversary theme with the late Catholicos Vazken I together with the Patriarchs of Jerusalem and Constantinople two years ago, to invite a group of scholars both Armenian and non-Armenian and have an open discussion with them about ways and means by which the seventeen centuries of our Christian heritage may be brought to world attention through scientific and academic circles.

Of course, much work has been and is being done in the study of Armenian history and culture. Indeed, we are deeply grateful for the work accomplished and the work in process not only in Armenia but also in the Diaspora.

Noravank Monastery, which is situated on a tributary of the Arpa River near the village of Areni in the Vayots Dzor region of Armenia, was restored during the reign of Catholicos Karekin I, under the sponsorship of Mr. and Mrs. Dicran Hadjetian.

The passing of His Holiness Vazken I, my election as Catholicos of All Armenians, then the election of Catholicos Aram I of the Great House of Cilicia, delayed the implementation of the idea. Last September when we had the first meeting in Etchmiadzin of the Central Committee for the 1700th anniversary, we decided to have this consultation in Paris as a first step in the course of planning and preparing events and activities that will take place between now and the year 2001 when we will mark the 17th centenary in a most solemn celebration in Holy Etchmiadzin.

I am delighted and thankful to you all for having responded to the invitation of the Executive Committee headed by Archbishop Mesrob Krikorian and Archbishop Mesrob Ashjian to participate in this scientific consultation of scholars. As we all know, there is much work to be done.

...

The challenge is before us. Let us take it seriously and with utmost love and responsibility. Your suggestions, your experience and your possibilities will enrich our endeavor. We consider you partners in our task. I thank you wholeheartedly and wish you the very best in your deliberations.

Address to the Consultation Conference, 1996

The year 2001, the first year of the third millennium, is a new dawn for the Armenian people. The entire nation, our Motherland—the re-established free Republic—as well as the Armenian community of the Diaspora, will

welcome this momentous anniversary and make it a part of their lives. A commemoration of this magnitude should not become, cannot become, an occasion for self-glorification. Rather, it must be an occasion for education and reflection, leading to true and profound self-recognition and an era of renewal in our personal and community life. Simply stated, we must ask ourselves, "Who am I as a member of the Armenian Apostolic Holy Church." This question must become the guiding and compelling force in our quest. "Am I simply an heir to that spiritual posterity that has 1700 years of multi-faceted and multi-valued richness, or am I one that has been given the privilege and responsibility to continue the legacy. And if I am to continue the legacy, I must first know what it is that I have inherited so that I can pass it on to the next generation enriched.
Pastoral Letter, uncirculated, 1999

How profound is the ancient proverb that says, "From the fires of the past, carry the flames, not the ashes." In this sense the past may turn into a force that may lead the young generation to a new *conscientization* of their identity as the torchbearers of the living and life giving flame of the Christian faith which has proven indomitable all along the past twenty centuries. The young are not only the inheritors, but, as I said, the torchbearers, a generation not to look backwards to the past for a sort of consolation or empty pride, but forward with new vigor and vision for greater achievements, to carry on forward the flame that gave life to their forefathers. Therefore, the 17th Centenary should be converted into a kind of Pentecost for the renewal of the Armenian Church.
Reflections on the 17th Centenary Celebration, 1999

THE FINAL JOURNEY

*D*eep in my heart, I feel that all of us present on this solemn occasion inaugurating this exhibition—an unprecedented event in its nature and scope—are not merely spectators of past achievements, but rather partakers in the history-building process.

I wholeheartedly and gratefully greet my beloved Brother in Christ His Holiness John Paul II, whose presence among us brings a unique and genuinely ecumenical spirit to this cultural event. I know well from my previous visits with His Holiness that from the early days of his youth in his beloved homeland of Poland, he has carried a special love and deep sympathy for the Armenian people, her Biblical land of Mount Ararat, her Apostolic Church, her cultural heritage and her struggle for justice.

I thank him for his global vision of Christianity, and for his spirit of openness and love for all humankind. May God grant him the blessings of good health for many years to come, to carry on his immense responsibilities in this special time that links together the Second and Third millennia of our common Christian history.

The "Rome-Armenia" exhibition being hosted by the Vatican Library speaks for itself; it needs no further comment. What I consider to be of special significance and worthy of bringing to international consideration is the 1700th anniversary of the official constitution of the Armenian Church, whose roots go back to the Apostolic Age. It is a tradition known around the world that in the Year of Our Lord 301, King Tiridates of Armenia and St. Gregory Partev, known as the Illuminator, proclaimed the Christian faith as the religion of the nation.

Since that time, for seventeen centuries, the Christian witness has been carried forward in the land of Armenia, and

*His Holiness' final journey from New York to Armenia,
via London and Rome where he attended the opening of the Vatican's exhibit
dedicated to the 1700th anniversary of Christian Armenia.*

within the life of the Armenian people throughout the world, without interruption, and in a spirit of deep faithfulness, endurance and perseverance.

This exhibition is one in a series of cultural activities being pursued in different parts of the world—similar exhibitions have already been held at the Kremlin in Moscow, in Athens, Greece, and in Helsinki, Finland—to make known, both to a new Armenian generation and to the world at large, the spirit and the value of these 1700 years of service to Christ, to His Church and to humankind. In my own understanding, what happened in 301 in Armenia was not an event confined to the borders of Armenia. It is part of the heritage of the Christian faith, and belongs in a pan-Christian, global context. The authentic nature of the conversion of Armenia is truly "ecumenical" in the literal sense of that word: it speaks to all people in the entire inhabited world.

As I have said in other contexts and in more elaborate ways, the 1700th anniversary celebration should be conceived and pursued in such a way that it may become a time of renewal for our Armenian Church, touching every aspect of our life as a people. Any Christian celebration is by definition a time for thanksgiving and humility, and not a time for boasting or self-glorification. The coming celebration is an opportunity to make us more cognizant of our predicament as Christians in the world of today.

The exhibition, too, provides us with an excellent opportunity to reflect more responsibly and creatively about our present-day role in making the past seventeen centuries of Christian witness a source of motivation for new achievements in the "vineyard of the Lord."

Clergy and friends joined the Pope and the Catholicos at the Vatican for the opening of the exhibit.

Indeed, had it not been for this paramount value of the 1700th anniversary, it would not have been opportune for me to undertake this journey to the Vatican under my present health conditions.

Nevertheless, I made a special effort to come, together with my beloved brother, His Holiness John Paul II, and joined by the high-ranking clergy representing the Hierarchical Sees of the Armenian Church, to signify the importance of these seventeen centuries of faithful service to the universal Christian Church, to the world at large, and to the Armenian people. It is a fact of history—certified by generations of Armenian martyrs—that this service has proved costly.

The fact that the celebration of the 1700th anniversary coincides with the first decade of a new era in Armenian history is indeed a development of great significance. The era of our free and independent state was proclaimed in the first year of the last decade of the 20th century, and the presence here at this exhibition of His Excellency Mr. Robert Kocharian, the President of the Republic of Armenia, is a heart-warming factor for all Armenians. Through this young republic, we can present ourselves to the world not as a nation under the domination and oppression of an alien system, but as one renewed in its vision through its regained freedom. May God's Name be praised.

Today, I cannot conclude this address without praying for peace in Kosovo. I hope that military action will be avoided.

Before concluding, I would like to express my heartfelt thanks and appreciation to all people, organizations and institutions that have shared in the concrete realization of this noble project: the authorities of the Vatican Apostolic Library, the Armenian Embassy at the Vatican, the Vatche and Tamar Manoukian Foundation, the Calouste Gulbenkian Foundation,

The Pope embraces His Holiness.

the Executive Committee of the 1700th Committee, and Professor Claude Mutafian, the dynamic scholar to whom we owe so much for his persevering efforts.

Now that the exhibition is open, I exhort our people to come forward and enter into communion with that distinctive spirit of creativity that has characterized our ancestors during the past centuries. As we prepare to cross the threshold of the Third Christian Millennium, let us respond by becoming the new and courageous torchbearers of that same spirit, for today and for the years to come.

Address at opening of the Vatican Library's "Rome-Armenia" Exhibit,
March 24, 1999

With these insights, as your spiritual father, and as the first servant to the Armenian Apostolic Church, I want to the best of my ability to address all of our people, without discrimination, with a monthly Pontifical Epistle, or letter. Through this communication I hope to explain the major aspects of our heritage and contributions, our church's religious beliefs and rituals, and acquaint you with our national treasures and the accomplishments of the past 1,700 years, so that there will be greater knowledge and closer ties to our Christian faith which has provided us with 1,700 years of riches and a strong foundation in the life of our nation.

...

His Holiness and Robert Kocharian, President of Armenia, join in the ribbon cutting, which officially opened the Vatican Exhibit.

I made this decision as a result of the last four months during my illness and weeks of treatment when I had the time to contemplate, to reflect, to meditate, to observe and analyze.... I offer these thoughts as a response to our people who have expressed warm love for the Armenian Apostolic Church, for her spiritual center, the Mother Holy See of Etchmiadzin, and because I sense their desire to become better acquainted with their Holy Church on the occasion of the 17th Centenary. I have said on many other occasions that the primary goal of the 17th Centenary commemoration is for the renewal and reawakening of our Church and the re-Christianization of our people through the teachings of our Lord's Gospel and the traditions of our Holy Apostolic Church.
Pastoral Letter, uncirculated. 1999

I consider myself fortunate to have loving and faithful friends and family. It is true that we humans see more clearly and appreciate what we have during the critical moments in our lives. And we also see clearly that life is God's gift...
Taped conversation, 1999

Mr. Vatche Manoukian presents a copy of the exhibition catalogue to Pope John Paul II.

Since my election to the Holy See of Etchmiadzin, I have enjoyed the companionship of my mother more than at any time in my life. You recall, I am sure...you were in Armenia at the same time in 1996 when my mother was also there. She would come during the spring and summer and stay with me. And in the autumn would not want to go home, but I feared that the winter months in Armenia would be too difficult for her and insisted that she return to Canada. Do you remember her saying that she was going to stay in Armenia no matter what I said? …. My illness has been hard on her although we have not told her exactly the nature and prognosis, nevertheless I think she senses that we are not being totally truthful….
Taped conversation, 1999

Back in Armenia, His Holiness receives a visit from James D. Wolfensohn, president of the World Bank, accompanied by Armen Sarkissian, former Prime Minister of Armenia, and Archbishop Karekin Nercessian, now His Holiness Catholicos Karekin II, Supreme Patriarch and Catholicos of All Armenians.

Joint Prayer

[Written in the hospital and recited together with young girl, 19 years old, suffering from a cancer like me]

Almighty and Everliving God
Our heavenly Father
As we are passing through hard moments
Of sickness and pain and agony
Together we raise our voice to the heavens
And say in unison:
Your name is love
Your love is everlasting
Your hope is inextinguishable.
We in humble obedience to your will
Put our trust in your grace and healing power.
We commit ourselves:
Whatever life you give us
We will always try to make it
Worthy to your love
And to put it to service to others
To the sick and the needy,
To the afflicted and the depressed
May your name be praised
For ever and ever. Amen.

Karekin I
Catholicos of All Armenians
11th February, 1999, New York

His Holiness's Final Message to the members of
the Brotherhood of the Holy See of Etchmiadzin:

Dear Brothers,
It is with deep spiritual sadness that I leave you to join my resurrected Lord. It is my wish that you remain in God's service for a long time; be brave and love the Mother See of Holy Etchmiadzin and keep her sacred spiritual and national mission alive. I am unbearably weak. May you remain strong.

With loving prayers,
Karekin I
18 June 1999
Holy Etchmiadzin

*I*t is difficult not to lose hope, I know. How can you maintain hope when you are losing every day? But, at the same time, when the hope is rooted in a sense of value, in an attachment to a faith, which is the backbone of our human existence, then the hope is not that kind of empty dreams, an ivory tower type of thing. The hope becomes part of our existence. I say, very simply, I have the hope to be awake tomorrow morning...."